BEYOND STICKY

BEYOND STICKY

Get off the commodity hamster wheel and create a bank brand people love.

MARTHA BARTLETT PILAND

Clovercroft/Publishing

Beyond Sticky

© 2019 by Martha Bartlett Piland

Published by Clovercroft Publishing, Franklin, Tennessee

Edited by Lee Titus Elliott

Cover Design by Gary Piland and Martha Bartlett Piland

Interior Design by Suzanne Lawing

Printed in the United States of America

ISBN 978-1-948484-78-7

ACKNOWLEDGEMENTS

With deep gratitude:

To Gary Piland, my greatest cheerleader
and the love of my life.

To Alexandra Reilly and Kristen Kögl, my groovy and wise
teammates who never shrink from a challenge.

To Mark E. McCormick, for his brilliant
insights and friendship.

To my wonderful parents and mentors,
Michael and Linda Bartlett.

Contents

IF YOU WANT TO FIND

INTRODUCTION

What really sticks, and what is just sticky?

Sticky can be good or bad: the sticky product a customer hates but feels there's no way to escape. Or the "I'm-stuck-on-you" relationship that's like true love.

If you're reading this book, you may be exhausted by the pace of constantly chasing the next deal, the next great employee, or the next rush of hot money that helps your ratios. You're tired of people perceiving you as a commodity when you know you have much more to offer than favorable rates or lower fees.

If you're reading this book, you may be looking for ways to make your institution more relevant.

If you're reading this book, you know you need to do something different.

You can be different in this ever-crowded, constantly changing marketplace. The sooner you get started, the better. It won't be easy. You'll have to trade some of your hamster-wheel energy for work that helps you move ahead, instead of simply running in place . . . feeling busy and exhausted, but not getting anywhere.

If you're reading this book, you need ideas that stick, not sticky old habits that keep you stuck in a loop. You want firm footing on a ladder taking you to new levels of customer loyalty and profitability, not pedals you labor to keep pushing, with no forward progress.

You may think these ideas can't be implemented, but think again. All you need is leadership, a strong team, shared values, and—stick-to-itiveness.

WHAT'S MY ROLE?

TO HELP YOU PLAN YOUR WORK AND WORK YOUR PLAN

Patrick Gideon, president of Silver Lake Bank, is one of my favorite bankers. He once said that hiring me was like hiring a personal trainer in marketing. I consider that high praise.

Personal trainers make their clients work hard: harder than they will on their own. Personal trainers challenge clients to follow a prescribed regimen, even when it seems daunting. And, together, they celebrate milestones and ultimate success.

My hope is that you'll use this book to challenge yourself and how you think about your institution. When you read, I hope you hear my voice cheering you on through those last, few, tough reps.

This book takes a holistic, strategic approach. It is not merely about advertising. It's about being a high-performance, high-value brand. It is broken into sections that interconnect many departments in your institution. Brand,

Culture, Customer Experience, Business Development and Business Innovation all working together will deliver powerful results and lasting change.

Now, drop and give me fifty!

MEET SAMMY HAMSTER

When I was a little girl, my brother Ted kept a tiny pet hamster, named Sammy, in a glass cage topped with a royal blue lid in his bedroom. Sammy had a shiny, silver wheel, plenty of toys, food, and water. My brother filled the bottom of Sammy's cage with fresh cedar shavings. Sammy loved to run on his wheel, often running for hours. Sammy was happy, and so was Ted.

It was still a cage.

One day, Sammy must have realized, like the rear sled dog, that unless you're the leader, the scenery never changes. He dreamed of freedom.

That day, he started to chew on the cedar shavings that lined his cage and to push them around into new arrangements. Soon, he'd jammed the shavings up under the wheel, locking it in place. And, with that, Sammy had transformed his wheel into a ladder. He easily climbed to the top of the wheel, reached the lid, and chewed a hole just large enough to escape.

And then he jumped.

Now free, Sammy had the run of Ted's bedroom and a vast new world.

Sammy had engineered a brave and innovative method of escape. Let him inspire you to get off your commodity hamster wheel that burns a lot of energy but takes you nowhere. It's time to push your organization around into new arrangements.

Let Sammy and this book help you reimagine your business and create a ladder that leads you up to your own vast, new world of opportunities and success.

GETTING THE BRAND TOGETHER

"Your brand is what other people say about you when you're not in the room."
—JEFF BEZOS, FOUNDER AND CEO OF AMAZON

"If you could taste words, most corporate websites, brochures, and sales materials would remind you of stale, soggy rice cakes: nearly calorie free, devoid of nutrition, and completely unsatisfying."
—JASON FRIED FOUNDER & CEO AT BASECAMP

"For me, my brand is good storytelling."
—LENA WAITHE, AMERICAN SCREENWRITER, PRODUCER, AND ACTRESS IN *MASTER OF NONE*

"Above all else, protect your brand. If you or your company doesn't live up to your brand's promise, own up to your error."
— JUDY SMITH, CRISIS MANAGER, AUTHOR, AND TELEVISION PRODUCER

FIVE KEY ATTRIBUTES OF A WINNING BRAND

A brand that delivers long-term revenue and profit does so because it has developed a sticky, emotional relationship with its fans.

When everything's right, it looks like this:

People **TRUST** a brand: they have come to expect that you'll deliver what you promise. You've built a relationship, and they believe what you tell them, until you break their hearts.

People are willing to **PAY MORE** for a brand: since they believe in you, they've come to expect that you're giving them something more. That willingness to pay more could be the currency of the time it takes to get there, how much money they spend, or the effort they exert to interact with you.

People **TALK ABOUT** brands: the grocery store, social media, the PTA meeting, online review sites . . . the list goes on. Both satisfied and dissatisfied people will talk. Do everything you can to ensure they're speaking favorably about you.

People like to be **ASSOCIATED** with great brands: the H-emblazoned handbag, the red-soled shoes, the distinctive, fountain-shaped hood ornament, and the logo-ed golf shirt are outward symbols of peoples' desire to be associated with their brands of choice. In those cases, they're actually paying to advertise for their beloved brands. What third-party endorsement could be better?

People are **LOYAL** to brands: people come back again and again, when you uphold your promise, value, and trust. That's the magic. Over a lifetime, its importance can't be overestimated. In the best circumstances, that loyalty can span generations. How many of us use a product our parents believed in?

BIRDS AND BRANDS: BOTH CAN BE SMALL AND MIGHTY

The first thing I noticed, as I looked out my kitchen window one cold winter morning, was that my bird feeders were nearly empty. A rush of guilt came over me, as I thought about how I'd procrastinated stopping at the hardware store for more birdseed.

But then I noticed something that made me smile. On the feeder closest to the window, I saw a tiny, buff-colored bird sitting on the feeder and—what? Feasting. That bird was so small she could fit more than half her body into the opening in the feeder. She was making a veritable feast of the seed that remained in the bottom. Most other birds would never be able to reach that food because they're just too big or they couldn't see it.

Can a sliver of a splinter turn into something so irritating that a customer goes somewhere else to find relief? Maybe all that's needed is a little care and nurturing—but like those unseen seeds, it has to be recognized in the first place.

That bird must have felt pretty pleased with herself. She saw an opening (literally) and seized a fine opportunity that fit her unique abilities.

My first reaction at seeing the "empty" bird feeders was to feel guilty. But the tiny bird reminded me of something I already believed. Noticing small details—and matching them with unique talents and attributes—can prove powerful. What might first feel like a losing situation can become your victory dance if you're present, and if you're paying attention.

How many times do brands overlook simple, seemingly insignificant details that can make a huge difference in their business? Those small things can either build or erode all their hard work.

You could be missing out on a feast. Are there some tiny details that you're overlooking? Find out now.

HOW EXCELLENT SERVICE DEVALUES YOUR BRAND

I repeat: they said they don't really need a loan, so they don't need to talk to a banker.

I recently asked a variety of C-level people how often they were called on by a banker trying to get their business. I heard one thing that surprised me—and it's not what you think.

Several said they don't really need a loan, so they weren't that interested in talking to a banker.

Wait. What?!

That means they think a loan is all a financial institution really has—or wants—to offer (sell) them. This concerns me because that means many bankers are positioning themselves as service-oriented, order-taking, wait-for-for-the-customer-to-ask kind of people. People who have money to loan.

You might be thinking, "Yes, this is pretty nice. We're proud of the world-class service we offer to people who come to us."

I'm here to tell you this is bad. It's worse than bad. This makes you and your institution a commodity. And it means you're relegated to lowest price positioning that never, ever engenders loyalty.

Your bankers need to get out on the front lines and have meaningful conversations. They need to be listening to the prospect's woes, then offering strategic ways to attack those woes at the source. What are the real answers that help drive more efficiency and profitability for that customer's business?

- Does the company deal with lots of individual payments? Then what if your institution can help them improve cash flow by collecting receivables faster?

- Perhaps the prospect has hundreds of unbanked employees. Can you simplify payroll processing with a pay-card or a FinTech solution that also helps protect their employees from expensive check cashers?

- Maybe your prospect is looking for ways to help lessen the burden of rising health insurance costs passed on to their employees. Can you help them with HSAs that will save employees on taxes?

The answer is probably complicated. It might be a loan, or it might be something else entirely. If you're willing to do the work, you can solve it. That makes you a banker people need to talk to.

Your counsel—coupled with your institution's products—can make positive bottom-line impacts on businesses. Give excellent service, but also give valuable counsel.

That gives you the power to launch far past the competition, because their bankers are also sitting behind their desks, waiting to politely answer the phone.

QUIT TELLING PEOPLE YOU HAVE CLEAN RESTROOMS

Too many institutions tout fast, local loan decisions and personal service as if they're the only ones who have it. Guess what? That's as effective as posting a sign that reads: "Clean restrooms."

Here are three ways to make sure you're presenting a better and—yes, unique—brand to your customers and prospects.

1. Steep your sales process and officer calling program in the brand.

Handing out mugs and other tchotchkes may be fine, but what you really need is people who can talk about your institution in unique, meaningful ways.

All employees need to know why your offerings are different, better, and important—and how their work contributes to making a difference for someone else.

What's the elevator pitch? It should be more than "quick, easy loan decisions" and "outstanding customer service." That's not your brand. That's an expectation as basic as a clean restroom at a restaurant.

Do all employees know about your prospects and who they are? What are the criteria for who you pursue? This is everybody's business, not just the business of the people with "sales" or "business development" on their business cards.

2. Add a brand-vangelist section to your internal communications.

Your internal communications vehicles are excellent places for brand information, standards, and protocols to be regularly shared. The employee handbook makes everything official, so addressing your brand there sends a message that it's vitally important.

Your intranet can provide continuous reminders and updates about what's happening:

- The brand promise
- The latest campaign
- New business wins
- Customer feedback
- Employee recognitions

Other smart places for communications: the employee break room, your internal social media, staff meetings, and lunch-and-learns.

These are simple ways to keep your brand promise highly visible, and employees enthused and engaged.

3. Designate a C-level person to oversee both marketing and HR.

When you ensure one person has responsibility to link people, purpose, and brand, it's far easier to connect the dots and make everything work together. Your purpose might be financial freedom, building communities, or independence. Do you just say it or really mean it?

Linking marketing and HR functions can help your entire organization really mean it. Recruiting, job descriptions, and performance evaluations can be connected to the brand promise and purpose.

Silos will be broken down—or avoided altogether. So when customers or prospects see an ad that makes a promise, they'll encounter staffers who really deliver upon it. Every single time.

Don't be a commodity.

People buying commodities buy on price. Build loyalty and profit by being better. Do the hard work of figuring out what's really different about your financial institution; then make sure all your employees know how to tell your story.

DO YOU LIVE YOUR SLOGAN, OR ARE YOU A COPYCAT BANK?

Nearly all financial institutions have a slogan. They believe it helps set them apart from competitors. And they think it's a key part of their brand. While that may be so, we see two big problems with a majority of these slogans: 1) they don't truly differentiate and 2) there's no real support behind the promise.

That's a big, bland problem.

Go to The Financial Brand website, and you can find a listing of 1,000 bank and credit union taglines.

Do they really differentiate?

Take a look: many sound very similar. They promise to pay attention to the customer or to be the hometown bank.

Yours might be there.

Of course, your color, logo, and slogan aren't the only things that comprise your brand. They're merely what make up the shorthand for your story. So while there may be some similar taglines, there's a real opportunity to take your visual identity and differentiate your institution by creating a unique story about what you offer—and living up to it.

Wear the shirt and walk the walk.

What does it mean to live out the slogan on a daily basis? It means that every employee inside your institution knows and embraces your purpose—and understands how to exemplify it.

This isn't just for public-facing employees. Everyone in your institution can be marketers and brand ambassadors if you give them the time and tools to help. It is far more than simply wearing a shirt with your logo. Here are some examples to inspire you right now:

If your slogan is "Keeping It Local" you could:

- Pledge to purchase supplies and services only from local vendors.

- Support the charities who keep their services and research local.

- Allow employees to volunteer on bank time to help local nonprofit organizations.

- Offer meeting spaces to local groups at no charge.

- Have a visible presence at local community events.

- Advertise on local media outlets—not just the big ones.

- Use your social media to show your support and give shout-outs about local happenings.

If your slogan is "Committed to World Class Service," you could:

- Have a concierge to assist bank clients with all of their financial needs.

- Offer twenty-four-hour access to safe deposit boxes.

- Go to the customer's location to sign loan papers instead of making her come to you.

- Train employees with the "Nordie" mind-set so they can deliver on the promise as needed.

- Dispense hand-sanitizing wipes at the drive-through.

- Provide transportation to your location for elderly or disabled customers.

If your slogan is "We Make Banking Easy," you could:

- Ensure your digital branch technology is second to none.

- Set up a five-minute switch kit for people to easily transfer bill pay and auto pay transactions to your institution.

- Prefill paperwork so that when you meet with customers, their time is kept to a minimum.

- Set up automatic approvals of safe deposit box and CD renewals.

- Don't charge for depositing checks by mobile phone.

It's easy to come up with ideas on your own. What's hard is establishing consistent actions that deliver the brand experience for every customer every time. While the marketing department might take the lead, this will require the efforts of a cross-functional team: HR, operations, and other departments must work together with marketing to make it happen.

If you develop brand experiences that truly differentiate your institution from your competition, your marketing ROI will exponentially grow. When you do, your brand will be worth more than its weight in gold.

HOW GOSSIP AMPLIFIES (OR MUFFLES) YOUR BRAND

Amazon Chairman Jeff Bezos has famously said, "Your brand is what people say about you when you're not in the room."

If you take this to heart, you need to understand all the people who talk about you when you're not in the room.

> Not only are they delivering water—they're also delivering news.

Sure, your customers talk. You're paying a lot of attention to them. Employees talk. I hope you're listening. One critical audience often overlooked is your suppliers.

Suppliers know more scoop than many of the famous celebrity-gossip columnists. They can make or break your brand with their talk to a multitude of listeners.

Those suppliers are often more than happy to share what they know—and it's likely to be more than you may realize:

- Who's slow to pay?
- Who's upset and jealous about their competition winning a new award?
- Who's firing employees faster than a politician in trouble?
- Who just won a big new customer?
- Who's launching something new?

Suppliers know all of this and more. It's easy for them to spread the word as they move from one office or phone call to the next.

What messages are you sending to suppliers—and what are they sharing with others? Be careful that your institution and your people don't become the subjects of an exposé.

Listen to what you're saying.

Pay attention to your interactions with suppliers at all levels.

- What are you saying in front of them?
- How are your employees interacting with them?
- Do you thank them for their hard work on your behalf?

Manage your verbal and nonverbal brand communications.

- Do you pay them fairly and on time?
- Are you respectful or dismissing?
- Are they invited to use your break room or restroom?
- Do you provide a convenient parking or loading area for them?

Testing, testing one-two-three.

I see it every day because I'm both a supplier and a purchaser. If you're in business, you are both, as well. Take a few moments to think about how you're treated—and how you treat everyone. Make sure those intentions and actions align with your brand.

Drop mic.

ALL FIVE SENSES CREATE A SUPERSTICKY, CAN'T-PUT-IT-DOWN BRAND

For many, branding involves only one or two sensory experiences. But brands that engage all five senses create something supersticky. Like double-stick tape, it's nearly impossible to put down.

Here are five ways to bond your brand to its fans.

1. See

It isn't just your logo or website. It's everything you do that visually communicates with both employees and customers.

Check the things that become like wallpaper, because you see them every day: signage, welcome mat, atrium, restrooms, employee apparel, fleet graphics, and parking lot. If you're fierce and high-performance, do they reflect that, or do they read "wimpy" instead? Be sure what people see is what you mean.

2. Smell

Movie theaters have it: the unmistakable smell of hot, buttered popcorn. Victoria's Secret stores have it: the signature fragrance that envelops shoppers when they walk in. One of my favorite banks wafts the smell of freshly baked cookies on people who walk in the door. Ooooh!

Imagine the smell of Play-Doh or Crayola crayons. Your experience of the brand is strongly linked to their unique scent.

Science has proven the power of smell and its ability to trigger emotional memories. Is there a way to use smell to make your brand more distinct and memorable?

3. Taste

Since you're not a food brand, you may struggle with this one. You still need your own proverbial flavor of brand Kool-Aid. Your flavor is that unique recipe of purpose, passion, and people that builds your brand from the inside out.

Are you a financial health brand? Then, help your people be healthy. Promote healthy conversation, activities, and actions that align with the vibrant face you want the world to see. You could offer insulated water bottles or a gourmet blend of herbal tea instead of run-of-the-mill coffee cups and pens.

4. Touch

The cover of *Fast Company* magazine has an unusual texture. Pick it up in the dark, and you'll immediately be able to identify it. Some consumer packaged goods also do this brilliantly.

How can you translate this concept to your own brand? Could it be the shape or paper of your business card or collateral materials? Handshakes, reception area furniture, and shipping boxes should also have your personal (branded) touch.

Bonus points for taking a look at your ATMs. Are the

touch pads dirty or clean? Don't leave your customers with a big "ICK!" reaction. Make it standard procedure for personnel to wipe off the key pads and touch screen each time they stock the machines with money and supplies.

> Service is not a position, and you've got to pay more than lip service to your brand.

5. Hear
A product jingle or that "wah" sound of the PlayStation are auditory brand cues. For financial brands, it could be the timbre of the voice that greets callers, your after-hours phone message, the music that plays in your lobby, or the ambient sounds of business. Do these build or erode your brand?

When was the last time you phoned your bank and listened to the on-hold music? Like many businesses, it probably hasn't been changed in years. And if the songs don't alternate, customers hear the same song every time they call. Stop torturing them. You can be better.

Don't wait to get supersticky.
Bond your brand to its fans. Every day that you work to be stickier and emotionally connected with employees, suppliers, board, and customers drives profit and builds loyalty that lasts.

HOW TO PAY MORE THAN LIP SERVICE TO YOUR BRAND
Many financial institutions struggle with differentiating themselves in this commodity–mind-set industry. "We need a new

slogan," they say. And they also say, "Let's talk about our fantastic service."

Here are some ways to set your financial brand apart, then pay it off with real-life, believable actions.

Make a pledge.

We worked with one bank to institute a four-pillar pledge:

1. ethical

2. adaptable

3. customer-centric

4. invested

With each of these values, there's a one-to two-sentence description of what it means. This pledge applies to all its audiences—customers, stockholders, and employees—so everyone knows what to expect.

A strong pledge brings unity of purpose for your brand.

The four-pillar pledge is posted in the lobby, on the website, and in the break room. It's memorable and repeatable. It drives decision making throughout the bank. They ask, "Does this action align with our values?" If the answer is no, it's a nonstarter.

Stake a claim.

Another institution we admire has created an internal rallying cry, "Be Bold!" Unafraid to step out of the traditional banking comfort zone, they're getting out in the community and surprising customers and prospects with new ideas that say, "I'm thinking about your business, and I'm ready to help you grow."

Bankers at this institution are each given a small budget and a lot of latitude to boldly go where no banker has gone before. They're being creative and getting noticed by surprising customers and prospects in ways that set them apart from their competition.

At staff meetings, they share the stories of what they've done and the new connections they've made. They encourage each other and collaborate on ways to venture further.

Demonstrate leadership.

When leadership is truly committed to a promise, it filters all throughout the organization. It means that when people interact with the institution—no matter which market they're in—the experience is designed to be consistent and authentic. Over time, the bank truly sets itself apart from the competitors in every marketplace it serves.

Be strategic.

To deliver results, you must be strategic. Both of these banks have clear parameters around what they're doing. You should, too:

- Know *why* you're doing this.
- Know *what* goals you're trying to reach.
- Know *how* you'll live out your promises.
- Know *who* you're building relationships with (you can't target everybody).

If your checking all the boxes, you're well on your way to a brand that's rock solid.

Yogi Berra probably said something like, "There's always time to make another correction, even after the game's over." And he would have been right. We have to be careful not to overanalyze and tweak our brands to death. If we do, nothing will ever be accomplished.

"GOOD ENOUGH" ISN'T GOOD ENOUGH FOR YOUR BRAND

I've seen an awful lot of brand ugliness lately. Ugly design, boring advertising, cheap quality, and slipshod work. It's pure laziness that creates lasting harm.

A "good enough" philosophy tells employees and customers a lot about your organization.

Here are three DON'Ts:

You don't let your brother cut your hair.

So why is it OK for him to design your logo or build your website if designing logos and building websites are not his professions? Saving money is an unacceptable reason. (This message is for major institutions, not just for de novo banks.)

You don't have to spend a gazillion dollars to create a professional-looking brand. But you do need to invest in quality marketing tools.

If you're a "Merle's Way Groj Sale" entrepreneur and

a hand-lettered sign appropriately reflects your business, you're on target. For everyone else: to establish credibility, you must invest. Otherwise, what you're doing to your brand is akin to self-slander.

You're tempted to do a "collab."

Currently, there's a huge trend, where major designers do a collaboration with a mass retailer like Target or Kohl's. Some call it "democratization" of fashion. This isn't isolated solely within the apparel industry, and I think all parties should be wary.

If you have to cheapen your offerings and cut important corners simply to sell more, you're playing a dangerous game. Suddenly, your "real" branded products don't seem as special to the people paying top dollar. And the cheap versions that are flimsy or falling apart disenchant the masses, too.

Eventually, you'll have no loyalty left, because your name and your product mean nothing.

You're tired, so you give up.

Last week, I found myself pushing a client to make refinements to an important communication before sending it out. After the second round of changes, he declared, "It's good enough," and off it went.

But it wasn't good enough. Customers will notice that something isn't quite right. It certainly won't be a good reflection on the brand to prospects.

Maybe what's most important: any employees who were part of the process see that the boss has a "good enough" mentality. And that's what they'll adopt. Soon, the acceptance of mediocre will spread through the organization like a virus. The brand will lose its luster and the distinct audience it used to attract. We can never get lazy and call our brand "good enough." The moment we do, hungry, ambitious competitors will go racing past.

PRACTICE MAKES PERMANENT: FOR MUSIC AND FOR BRANDS

You've heard the expression, "Practice makes perfect." Esteemed music professionals will tell you a better motto is, "Perfect practice makes permanent."

Here are their words of wisdom for bankers who want their businesses to perform like rock stars.

Preach what you practice.

The gospel of your brand deserves your very best. Your actions speak louder than words. Employees will see what you do and emulate your actions. Those actions are far more powerful—and credible—than words alone.

Don't cut corners.

Lazy practices deliver poor performance. Just ask any famous musician. Superstars achieve success with the daily discipline of doing things right every single time. The right actions become second nature, and mistakes become rare. Be sure your employees have excellent coaching so they're not tempted to take shortcuts. Help them become high-performance contributors to your success.

Use the same songbook.

You already know everyone needs to be on the same page.

But is everyone singing the right part?

Together, there's harmony, but a few wrong notes create very noticeable discord. The same with your brand: a disgruntled employee griping to her neighbor or a well-intentioned one giving bad advice to his customer are equally dangerous.

Make sure you're communicating expectations clearly and regularly.

Don't just pay your brand lip service. Help your employees with regular training and reinforcement. The rest will be music to your ears.

CREATING THEATRE FOR YOUR BRAND, AND WHY IT MATTERS

A blockbuster brand has all the elements of Broadway-worthy theatre. Creating drama, pageantry, and excitement with both employees and customers generates raving fans, who are eager to tell others.

Do you have all the elements to create a legendary brand?

Here's your checklist.

Script

Your script is your messaging, talking points, elevator speech, and recruitment materials. It's your story, and it should be filled with drama, color, and purpose. It is foundational to all the other elements of your production.

Director

The CEO is the leader with the vision that directs others. The director sets the tone, then makes the artistic and technical decisions that tie everything together seamlessly. The tone gets hearts pounding and people cheering. But, without that vision and direction, the production—and the brand—flounder.

Cast

Every frontline employee is integral in telling the story. Each has a vital role to play: doing and saying the right things at the right time. Rehearse, reinforce, and make it flawless. When all know their parts—either leading parts or supporting ones—sales efforts are fruitful. Customer service seems effortless, and profits grow.

Crew

These are the employees who are behind the scenes who are making everything work, as if by magic. They also help the story unfold, and they're every bit as important as the cast. Silently in the wings, they ensure that props are in place and that the scenery and set pieces appear on cue. Like the cast, they are well-rehearsed. Because of them, the technology works, orders are filled, customers are wowed, and word of mouth grows.

Stage

Well-crafted lighting, set design, props, costumes, and music can leave an audience breathless. Your product or service should be presented with similar fanfare. The result: employees are energized, and customers are enraptured. When you create this kind of excitement, you keep the audience on the edge of their seats, wanting more.

Don't forget the cast party.

You need to give cast and crew regular feedback: how to improve their performance and how magnificent they were.

Let them enjoy the limelight for all their hard work. Then do it all again.

Are your audiences begging for more? Approach your brand as if it's a major theatrical production. We're confident you'll be answered with critical acclaim.

"What's crucial in a High Street store is a compelling reason for people to shop there. Shops must offer excellent customer service—and 'theatre' is a must."
—THEO PAPHITIS

YOUR BRAND'S MOST IMPORTANT SIGN: THE EXIT

There's a lot of talk about displaying welcome mats and rolling out the red carpet for customers. But are you also taking care of them on the way out? Here's a three-way checklist for asking the right questions.

1. Customers
• Once you've acquired them, have you tried to keep them? Or did you get lazy and take them for granted?

- How do they feel on the way out? Did you do your job? How did you make them feel? Will they tell others?

- Are they exiting just for today—or are they exiting for good? How do you know?

2. Employees

- If they leave your employment (voluntarily or involuntarily), how are they treated on the way out?

- When they leave for the day, do they feel pride in work well done? How do they talk about you to their family and friends?

- Do they know your purpose, vision, and mission, or are they outsiders?

3. Prospective employees

- Do you share your purpose, vision, and mission and draw them in?

- Does someone escort them to the door and warmly thank them for their time?

- When you've made your hiring decision, do you let all of them know promptly—or do you string them along?

- If they're not hired, do you let them down gently and thank them again for their time—or do you send them a soul-crushing form letter?

You've heard the expression, "Don't let the door hit you on the way out." Be sure your brand isn't the one being sent packing.

CHOOSY BRANDS CHOOSE GROUCHO–RIGHT?

Groucho Marx is famously quoted as resigning from the Delaney Club, quipping, *"I wouldn't belong to any club that would have me as a member."*

Whether or not the story is actually true, it leads us to wonder why some brands are so eager to accept just anyone.

The quick fix that's addiction in disguise.

Taking just anyone is like the sugar buzz that gives you a quick high but then lets you down hard. It can happen just about anywhere:

- Taking the first job applicants for the position because they seem eager, bright, and shiny. But upon closer inspection—when it's too late—you realize they were just put-ons. They don't embrace your internal brand, and what you thought was love for your purpose was love for the idea of a paycheck and little else.

- The new influx of members attracted by the discounted offer who turn out to be overly demanding and a bad fit with the tried-and-true members. The discounted newbies never really join in, or worse, they gobble up your resources, then drift away when the next big thing is offered somewhere else. (By then, you're glad they're gone, but they've hurt your reputation.)

- The CD special that gives your bank a temporary flush of fat new deposits. But this hot money lasts only as long as the term and the promotional rate. There's no loyalty, just the desire for a quick buck. When the offer expires, the money is gone—and so are those customers.

- The lure of a big retail promotion that offers a deep discount or a gift with purchase. It can bring in a rush of revenue at key times. But do it too often, and the luster of the brand becomes tarnished. The original customers may move on to find something else that's really valuable.

Pick your poison.

Reward best customers and attract quality prospects by selectively using specials and sales promotions.

Would Groucho be a good fit for your brand? His personality might attract more of what you really want, or it might cause a deadly overdose.

Never favor quantity over quality, because that devalues both aspects of your brand: internal and external. If you're willing to sacrifice the fleeting in favor of the long-term, you'll build loyalty and profit.

TEN THINGS OFTEN OVERLOOKED IN A BRAND AUDIT

Keeping your brand aligned means regularly auditing everything that tells your story.

What's in sync? What's at odds with the brand? It's easy for elements to slowly stray away. The causes can be lack of a good brand standards guide or employees being unaware of it (or ignoring it). Sometimes, it's what we call Brand Fatigue: your internal team members get weary of the rules of consistency and decide to take things into their own hands and make changes they prefer.

Whatever the cause, a regular audit helps ensure consistency at all times, through all media.

And while you must evaluate advertising and PR messages, you should never overlook the many other things that speak loud and clear.

Here's a starting checklist of additional things to monitor for your public-facing brand:

1. **After hours phone greeting and on-hold music:** the last time you phoned and listened was...? It's probably been ages. Call. Listen. Update.

2. **Email sig:** this is free advertising! Is everyone in your organization using the same format that builds your brand? This is no place for individual flair and comic sans.

3. **Reception area:** customers, delivery people, suppliers, and many others are there every day. How are they greeted, and what do they see, smell, hear, touch, and taste? Do all their senses perceive the brand message you're trying to convey?

4. **Restrooms:** the cleanliness, lighting, tidiness, decor, and maintenance of your restrooms send a clear signal about how you manage other aspects of the brand. This is for everyone, not just restaurants.

5. **Business cards:** stop giving people crummy business cards. Use good paper and quality printing. A thin, dog-

eared card makes it look as if you don't care about your people or who they serve.

6. **Fleet graphics:** your fleet should be clean, shiny, and looking sharp. Vehicles are roving billboards that make a powerful impression for better or for worse. Bonus points for having safe, courteous drivers.

7. **Swag:** get rid of those mugs, pens, and cozies with your old logo. I know they cost money. But continuing to pass them out dilutes your brand equity. Donate them to a charity in another part of the world where you don't do business. Or toss them. Now.

8. **Signage:** there's a financial services firm in our neighborhood that does some amazing work. Sadly, its outdoor sign is partly obscured by shrubbery, and its logo is peeling and faded. Though many of the firm's clients are out of town, the locals may perceive that this institution is struggling. The world is too small to let people think you're anything but prosperous. This is especially true when they're thinking of how you're handling their money.

9. **Parking lot:** freshly painted stripes and "welcome visitors" or "reserved for hard-working moms" signs make people feel good. They make a first impression—or a repeated impression—about how you feel about the people coming to see you.

10. **Social media:** besides your Instagram, Facebook, and the other usual suspects, take a look at review sites, online Yellow Pages listings, and employment sites. Is your logo current? Have you claimed and populated

accounts with good information? Google yourself and look past the first few listings. Dig in and find out what needs attention.

Everything speaks.
Make sure your messages are in unison.

It's not just one and done.
Most likely, you have multiple branches, a digital branch, ATMs, and an app. Be sure you're auditing everywhere, not just at the places closest to you. Since it's easy to overlook things you see every day, you might consider having bankers from one location secret-shop a different branch. This is a good way to make some new discoveries and deeply involve your people in this important assessment.

THREE KINDS OF HOARDING THAT SMOTHER YOUR BRAND

Look into the proverbial closet of your organization. Chances are there are a few habits or tactics you know you need to give up. For some reason, you just can't make yourself do it. Worst-case scenario: you have a vast storehouse that needs to be purged by Marie Kondo right away.

What's still hanging around is weighing you down. It's a sign of sickness that needs immediate intervention.

Here are three kinds of hoarding that hurt your brand:

1. Clinging to too many messages.
You can't be all things to all people, and you can't give them ten reasons to like your brand.

You need one simple message. In a pinch, people can remember a one-two-three. But more than that? Your brand voice just adds to the clamor assaulting people from all sides.

In trying to say everything, you say nothing.

Be disciplined to find—then amplify—your One True Message. This will help your organization grow and prosper.

2. Failing to let bad customers go.

They're the ones who complain about everything. The fee is too high, and the product is lacking. They're dissatisfied at every turn. They're slow payers or, they have frequent overdrafts. Maybe they mistreat your employees. Most likely, they're bad-mouthing your brand to others.

Why are you hanging on to them? Fear of losing their revenue is not an excuse.

Purge these oxygen suckers from your customer list so you can devote positive energy to growing new business and nurturing relationships with current high-value customers. Morale will improve. And so will your bottom line.

3. Resisting tossing away outdated materials.

Is your storeroom filled with envelopes bearing logos retired ten years ago? Are you still hanging on to that box of folders with your old tagline because they were expensive? Are you still giving away outdated corporate swag?

This does not send a message that you're frugal. It sends confusing and mixed messages about who you are and what you stand for. It makes you look tired, cheap, and irrelevant.

Your brand deserves a clear, compelling message. Sweep out the cobwebs, and see the bright, attractive, new you in the marketplace. You'll bask in the glow of more revenue and profit.

Often, less is more. Streamline and create room for your institution to flourish.

CULTURE IS NOT JUST FOR PETRI DISHES AND YOGURT

*"With the right people, culture, and values,
you can accomplish great things."*
—TRICIA GRIFFITH, PRESIDENT AND CEO
OF PROGRESSIVE INSURANCE

*"A single person doesn't change an organization,
but culture and good people do."*
—FRANCES HESSELBEIN, FORMER GIRL SCOUT CEO AND
PRESIDENTIAL MEDAL OF FREEDOM HONOREE

*"Corporate culture matters. How management chooses to treat
its people impacts everything—for better or for worse."*
—SIMON SINEK, AUTHOR OF START WITH WHY

"Culture drives great results."
—JACK WELCH, FORMER CHAIRMAN AND CEO
OF GENERAL ELECTRIC

YOUR CULTURE AND WHY IT'S CRITICAL

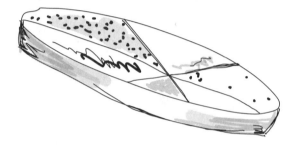

Corporate culture, like mold, will grow anywhere. It starts from tiny spores and replicates rapidly. Nature abhors a vacuum, so a culture will grow on its own if none is already established. In the absence of a conscious plan, something milquetoast at best—or virulent at worst—will take hold and start reproducing. The resulting infestation could sicken your bank, and eventually your customers, faster than you can imagine.

A few years ago, we worked with an institution that was rife with a nasty culture virus. While interviewing employees, we observed people literally looking over their shoulders to see who might overhear them. They exchanged sideways glances with one another in group meetings. They worked for a bullying, midlevel micromanager, and they were afraid. The president chose to look the other way.

Contrast that with a different bank leader who trusts and empowers the staff. They have power (within stated parameters) to make decisions that delight customers. They ask themselves, "How does this work affect my customers?" and they act accordingly. This bank's president has planted the seeds for a flourishing institution. Everyone—customers and employees alike—can feel it when they walk into the bank.

You must have a conscious plan for creating a culture that supports a true mission and purpose. That's the key to cultivating a "stuck-on-you" brand for customers and the superstar employees you need to prosper.

STOP HIRING TELLERS: YOU NEED LISTENERS

The moniker "teller" has been around in banking since time immemorial. And while it may feel comfortable to you, it sends unintended messages. It positions banker relationships as one-sided—with the bankers holding all the power and the customers taking what's doled out.

You can be better. Here are three ways to get started.

Change the name and set the tone.

Get rid of the title and set a new tone for the relationship.

How do you want customers to feel when they interact with your team? We love the idea of *Listener versus Teller*. It signifies someone who's paying attention and ready to help.

Live the listen.

You can't just change the name: you've got to back it up with action.

Work across your organization with Marketing, HR,

Operations, and other departments to train all employees on how to really listen to customers—and each other. For example:

- If there's a customer-service complaint, how do staffers listen first, then attempt to resolve?

- If a customer is stuck in the same, old, wrong-fit account, how do employees ask questions, listen, and recommend a better solution?

> "We have two ears and one mouth so that we can listen twice as much as we speak."
> —Epictetus, Greek Stoic philosopher

- If a prospect needs a loan, how are employees listening between the lines so they can offer the best options?

You probably need some role-playing exercises in the training. Allow your staff to bring up real-life examples of what they've encountered; then work on different approaches as a group.

Hire and evaluate better.

From the outset, establish your expectations that all bankers listen before talking.

Observe how prospective employees act in interviews.

- Are they eager to tell, or do they listen and then tailor their answers appropriately?

- Do they ask questions of you to better understand your brand, your expectations, and goals?

Take time to listen to the conversations going on around your bank or credit union.

- Are your employees truly listening during customer interactions?
- Do team members listen to each other when working on solutions?
- Are you really listening to employees when they approach you with ideas and challenges?

Notice the language and the actions so you can reward the desired listening behavior and coach for improvement where it's needed.

Watch your language.

Language is funny. People often live up to their label, usually without even realizing it. Reinvigorate the customer experience with your brand by ensuring that everyone is listening first.

EMPLOYEES ARE THE REAL POWER BROKERS OF YOUR BRAND

You probably work very hard to craft a consistent brand message through all your advertising, PR, and social media. And while that's important, it only takes you so far.

The real power brokers of the brand are employees. They can help build the brand—or torpedo it.

Who controls your brand?

Think about who has the power to create messages and experiences around your brand:

- you

- your employees

- your customers

In the graphic below, there's a sampling of the ways each constituent can affect what others think, feel, and say about your bank. In nearly every case, employees have the most control of the delivery of the brand promise to customers.

BRAND TOUCHPOINTS

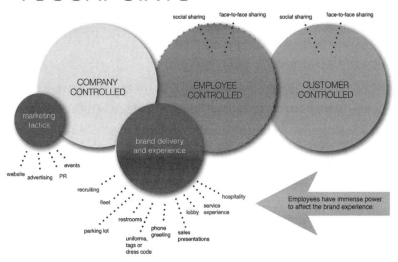

While company leadership may dictate a specific way something should be done, it's left up to each individual employee to carry it out.

What's happening at your bank?

Take a look around. Do employees know their important

role in helping to build the brand, to earn trust, and to sell? (Yes, everyone is a salesperson.) How do you know?

And if they do know their role, are they doing it the branded way? Do the lobby areas, phone greetings, dress code, sales materials, and in-person and online interactions all align with the principles of your brand? For example:

- If you're a top-tier bank, does everything you (and employees) put forth convey a top-tier image?
- If your brand promotes financial health and wellness, do you promote that to your employees and help them achieve it themselves?

But wait, there's more!

The chart above is a good starting point to analyze your brand's touchpoints. But it just scratches the surface. You may also need to consider:

- Sounds (music, conversation, ambiance)
- Smells (What should it smell like when people experience your brand?)
- Condition (i.e., shabby, sharp, spiffy, brand-new, polished)

No matter what details end up on your list, notice how many of them are affected by your employees, or your employees plus you.

What you need:

Training, ongoing communications, and modeling are critical elements. You also need:

- A kickoff and follow-up training meetings

57

- A "here's how we do it" manual
- Intranet messages
- Internal contests
- Internal videos
- Brand criteria incorporated into performance reviews
- ... and more

Anyone else?

In some organizations, other powerful controllers of the brand could be suppliers, advisory board members, and boards of directors.

Make sure you're paying attention to them, too.

Employees can help you get there.

Developing a new logo or marketing campaign can be a fine strategy. To make it really work, all employees must believe and act to help power your efforts and create success and profits.

AN AD CAMPAIGN WON'T FIX WHAT'S WRONG WITH YOUR TEAM

It's an all-too-common malady: sales are flabby or customer service goals are lagging, so leadership determines that a fresh new advertising campaign is just the thing to make everything right again.

When we start asking questions to diagnose the situation, we often discover something else: an internal problem.

You may be too close to the situation to see it. But one or more of these reasons could be at the heart of the matter:

- Your bankers need training.
- You need to get out of your staff's way.

The truth is that, in this case, an ad campaign is an expensive way to fix the wrong problem.

- Your staff members don't have the tools they need.
- You have staff members who aren't a good match for the jobs they're assigned.
- Your board members aren't behind you.

You may not like it when we tell you this, because an ad campaign seems like a much easier solution. It's fun. It's glitzy. It beats restructuring personnel.

There's nothing wrong with a new campaign. A sales promotion or brand refresh may be just what the doctor ordered. If you start with a strategic foundation, you can use it to drive traffic, build your customer base, or generate trial.

But before you consider a new external campaign, invest in an internally focused campaign that ensures all your employees—not just salespeople—know your message, your why, and your reasons to believe. Your job is helping them succeed.

Step one
Give them a shot in the arm. They need:

- Talking points
- Training and a chance to practice
- Tools like presentations, handouts, and memorable, branded tchotchkes

- Stretch goals

- A pep rally

- Regular communications with benchmarks toward progress

Step two

Once your internal rehab is well underway, everyone is healthy and ready for your outwardly focused campaign. They'll make your investment in that campaign go so much further you won't believe your eyes.

THREE BETTER WAYS TO LAUNCH YOUR NEXT AD CAMPAIGN

It's time for an update. You've held the focus groups, shopped the competition, and worked with your agency to create a message that truly differentiates your institution from all others. One caveat: don't launch it to customers and the public without a memorable premier for your most critical audience: employees.

Every successful financial institution—whether it's launching a CD special, a new ad campaign, or a brand overhaul—includes and involves employees before it shows anything to outside audiences.

Taking the extra steps to involve employees along the way—and capture their hearts by giving them the first look—ensures that the effort will have real momentum.

Here are some of our favorite examples of brand-launch events that captivated employees and built business.

Break the ice.

The CEO of one bank we worked with wanted to make a big impression on his bankers when he introduced the new brand at their annual meeting. We had an ice sculpture of the old logo wheeled out on a cart. After a few introductory remarks, the CEO pulled out a sledge hammer from behind the podium and smashed the sculpture to smithereens.

Needless to say, everyone's attention was riveted on him and what he would say next.

The message was clear. We're demolishing an old logo, and also an old way of doing business.

As he outlined the vision for new direction for the institution, its business, and the marketing plans, bankers were hanging onto every word. Before they recovered from their surprise, he went around the room with oversized scissors and, one by one, cut off their ties.

By the end of the meeting, everyone knew where they were going. They felt like insiders. And they were charged up and ready to make the new vision into reality.

Drink your own Kool-Aid.

Another bank we know launched a new brand campaign for its internal culture, because it wanted to amp up its already-strong customer-service game and turn it into something legendary.

We worked with the bank to create a service promise that grew out of employee input.

The Five-Point Promise was a commitment of what employees would do for bank customers. What's even more exciting: a Five-Point Promise from the management about what it would do for employees.

Plans were communicated through coffee-and-cookie staff meetings at the individual branch level. A visit and presentation from the president on how the program was developed—and the critical input that came that originated from employees—helped everyone feel valued and heard.

The service promise is now delivered inside and outside the institution, much to the delight of employees and customers.

Throw out the cookie cutters.

When another financial brand wanted to launch its new business plan and marketing campaign to employees, multiple locations separated by large distances made it impossible to bring everyone together in one place for a presentation.

So we worked with the chief marketing officer to create separate launches in each of their locations across the country. She enlisted the help of the office managers in each branch. It was a smart idea, because having the office managers as allies meant that the logistics of changing stationery, supplies, templates, email signatures, and myriad other outdated items would be much easier.

It was the office managers who decided whether the launch in their office would be done over lunch, over breakfast, or at some other time of day. They each had budget authority to choose newly branded swag, food, and everything they needed to orchestrate a memorable event. We provided a newsletter with a personal greeting from the CEO and talking points for that location's VP. There was also intranet content and other communications so that each event had consistency in message delivery.

Employees were wowed. The institution's leadership team received overwhelmingly positive feedback about the new brand, the company goals, and the means of learning about them. What's better: employees felt more connected to their colleagues in distant offices, which began to foster more cross-pollination of ideas and cross-selling of products and services.

Roll out the red carpet.

All of these institutions are reaching or exceeding their lofty goals. They have enviable cultures and are recognized market leaders. They roll out the proverbial red carpets because they recognize the importance of growing their brands from the inside out.

These leaders also know that internal brand engagement isn't a once-only activity. They continue to monitor, to encourage, to report results, and to coach. They're in it for the long term.

Building employee enthusiasm and deep awareness of the employees' important role in your organization's success is powerful. It creates advocates who propel your brand ahead for lasting results.

HOW GREEK RITUALS LEAD TO VICTORIOUS BRANDS

Animal House is probably the quintessential frat movie of all time. The outlandish actions of the Deltas are wildly exaggerated, but, even so, they have important lessons for any brand: especially one on Double Secret Probation. Here's what the Deltas can teach you and your bankers.

Throw a toga party.

The Deltas know they're in trouble. Instead of getting disheartened by dwelling on the nearly impossible odds of beating the fanatical dean, they throw an epic party that's one for the record books.

Every leader needs to periodically offer time out for fun. It boosts morale and gives people another burst of energy that can move the organization to the next level. It doesn't have to be expensive; it just has to be well conceived and aligned with the culture and the brand.

Invent a secret handshake.

Whether it's a secret handshake or some other ritual, like a certain style of high five or a silly victory dance, little rituals like these add up to something big, especially in times of trouble.

Such rituals help cement connections and camaraderie inside the organization.

They can be as simple as a quick time-out to cheer on a colleague, or something more elaborate that makes a big celebration even bigger and better. They say "you belong."

Use a full range of rituals.

All high-performance fraternities and sororities have consistent rituals they repeat regularly that keep them strong. Every organization should.

Here are a few rituals to make a regular part of your operations:

- Founder's Day—celebrate your roots.
- Reciting the pledge—knowing and honoring your mission.
- Initiation—have a best-in-class onboarding program.

- Wear the letters—wear and display your company logo with pride.

Don't allow yourself to be blindfolded.

Dissatisfied customers and grumpy employees will eventually land any brand on Double Secret Probation.

While many are blind to it for a while, it eventually becomes seen in the form of lagging sales, loss of loyalty, and employee turnover. Don't let this happen to you. Instead, build a strong culture that regularly celebrates its common ideas, ideals, and interests.

If you want a feeling of friendship and mutual support within your institution, take a few cues from fraternities. Creating your own secret handshakes and toga parties can lead to stronger teams and over-the-top ROI. Get started, and keep the rituals going. The resulting profit and revenue will make you want to shout!

YOUR BANK NEEDS A CAMPFIRE, NOT A WATER COOLER

Companies everywhere have a proverbial water cooler. It's the place to chat about sports or a new Dilbert-esque project handed down from above. Yawn. The special ones—high-growth institutions who rely on innovative employees—have a roaring campfire.

The watercooler atmosphere is a lot like treading water. Low energy. Chilly. Maybe, it breeds a little negativity. The campfire, on the other hand, is the place to come together. It's where people sing songs, roast marshmallows, and tell stories.

What's your lore?

Every company has a story. How did the company start? What were the founders thinking? Did their funding come from investors, an acquisition, or family assets? What is the underlying purpose?

Rapidly growing banks are writing new stories every day. There are fresh achievements, challenges to beat, and more than a few near misses. "Remember when the dog crashed through our window?" "How about the big win we made in the early years competing against the Goliath bank?" The triumphs are exhilarating. This is part of your lore.

As the institution grows, the new people who come on board haven't experienced the same history. Unless someone takes the time to tell them—and really draw them into the magic—they'll never be as connected to the brand as the original team. A strong internal brand keeps moving the company forward. So the new people need to drink the Kool-Aid (the hot chocolate?) so everyone's moving ahead together.

Rediscover s'mores with your team.

Here's the recipe: One large marshmallow, one large graham cracker, one-half of a Hershey bar. Heat the marshmallow over an open flame until it begins to brown and melt. Break the graham cracker in half. Sandwich the chocolate between the cracker halves with the hot, melted marshmallow. Wait just a moment for it to cool; then dig in. Enjoy!

Do you have a place to gather?

Besides telling stories, you need a place for people to bond. They need to feel safe. That's when they feel free to make up silly song lyrics and dream the dreams that lead to big ideas and innovations. This sense of place can be digital or physical. Ideally, it's both.

Consider changing up your break rooms or setting aside specific conference rooms to invite brainstorming and different, better thinking.

Create some online sharing tools, an intranet, and some internal social media to foster branded, purposeful fun and work.

Everyone loves a camp fire.

In the daily rush, never forget to carve out time for team-building retreats, group picnics, or planning sessions. Celebrate successes and spot the next thing to conquer together. Reinforce the love of the brand and why it matters. Use these times to build camaraderie and to keep everyone focused on the goals.

I hope your bank—on the inside and the outside—is like a crackling fire and the invitation of s'mores: impossible to resist.

YOUR BULLETIN BOARD IS LIKE A CANARY IN A COAL MINE

Obligatory rules and regs and a so-called motivational poster in a company break area make me think of some Despair, Inc. lampoons. The other stuff that's posted (or not) can signal an alarm about the health of the organization's internal brand.

You may think your internal brand is just fine. But how do you really know? If you're a rapidly growing or recently blended institution, you may not have slowed down lately to consider this question. But you must, because it's so closely linked to most other performance measures.

Ask "The Fixer."

My friend, Terry Harbert, is almost legendary in professional circles. He earned the nickname "The Fixer" because he knows how to go into an organization, spot the source of problems, and—well—fix them. Terry says one of his diagnosis tools is to go straight to the organization's bulletin boards and observe what's there.

He looks to see if it's merely full of DOs and DON'Ts, penalties, policies, and procedures. If so, he says there are probably some Dilbertlike forces at work. Those forces of darkness are putting the skids on innovation, love of the brand, and great performance.

Is the bulletin board locked up under glass?

I hope not. That means that the leadership is speaking, but not listening. And it reeks of suspicion and distrust.

Does it have personality and purpose?

If the bulletin area has some life and personality to it, that's a good sign. I asked Terry what he thinks should be on a healthy organization's board.

His hit list:

- Mission statement—and "not something stuffy, but something people really get and like."

- Employee recognitions from both inside and outside the company.

- A place for employees to list things they care about, like fund-raisers or even "for sale" items.

- Information about training opportunities.

That got me to thinking about our own bulletin board. Some other things we like to post:

- Articles or smart ads we've torn from magazines.

- Clips from laudable PR mentions about our firm.

- Photos of our staff at celebrations or performing community service.

- Congratulatory notes we've received from clients and friends.

- Cartoons that make us smile.

- Calendar with company and community events.

Of course, bulletin boards can be virtual, as well as old-school. We think having both is smart. Facebook, Pinterest, and Instagram are easy, fun ways to create a virtual bulletin board that everyone can enjoy. You can even create private boards so that you can keep this information for insiders only. The social tools are especially good if you want to unite employees who work in different locations.

If you're recruiting, a virtual bulletin board can be powerful.

High-growth companies who are recruiting stellar talent can give their prospects a view of their internal culture with a public board. Encouraging employees to post to the corporate page will allow their love of the brand and purpose to shine.

You can't fake that, and it can be incredibly exciting!

Take the time to diagnose.

Obviously, multiple strategies are needed. The bulletin board isn't the one magic pill to feed your internal brand. But it certainly can act like the proverbial canary if you take the time to listen for the song.

FRUIT BOWLS AND BRANDS: BEWARE THE BURIED BLEMISH

At the bottom of the fruit bowl, out of sight, a tiny blemish starts to fester. On top, everything looks beautiful and healthy. But, eventually, an odor develops. By the time you investigate—and actually find it—it has spread.

Brands that are rapidly growing can find themselves in this fruit bowl. Small bruises—hidden by the hustle of daily work—can grow into pervasive problems that can spoil everything around them unless you act quickly.

Here are six examples of sore spots to watch:

1. A disgruntled employee sowing the seeds of discord and whipping your culture into a negative frenzy.

2. A customer complaint on social media like Yelp! is left languishing and unaddressed.

3. A missing link in your business process slows production and interrupts prompt service.

4. The disengaged board member who doesn't know your purpose and vision, so he makes up a script of his own.

5. The silos within the company that create an "us-versus-them" mentality, so people are fighting or jockeying for position instead of pulling you forward together.

6. The micromanaging branch president creating fear and paralysis.

Act quickly. If caught early, all you have to do is remove the offending piece and do a light cleanup.

But left unattended, the nastiness will spread to others within your circle. Soon, customers and the community will hear of it. You'll have a lot of waste and some very distasteful work to do.

Don't ignore them. They will never go away on their own.

But if you catch them early, you're well on your way to serving up an apple-a-day brand.

FROM GROAN TO GREAT: MAKING YOUR NEXT RETREAT THE BEST ONE YET

Be honest: have you ever heard an employee (sincerely) say "OH cool—I'm so excited!" when you announced an all-staff company retreat? For many, the thought of a day away from the bank stuffed into a meeting room to plan sounds like as much fun as a root canal.

The lack of enthusiasm may come from a number of traumatic past experiences:

- New ideas were shot down or ridiculed.
- The retreat was poorly planned, so the day felt rushed or unimportant.
- A few people talked—a lot—so other opinions were never heard.
- Innovative new plans had no follow-up or support after the retreat, so they fizzled out.

Here are smart ways to get people smiling and moving your organization forward together.

Have a goal.
Having a retreat just because it's a yearly event isn't good enough. Why are you gathering? How will you measure the outcomes of your retreat? Define these things first.

Create a theme.
Set the tone for your retreat with a theme that supports your event goals and your organization's purpose. Is it serious, festive, or all-hands-on-deck? Setting the tone helps manage expectations so that participants arrive in the right frame of mind—and with a shared vision.

Send an invitation.
An Evite or a paper invitation is the second part of setting the tone. It shows that the retreat is important. Let people know the agenda, how they should dress, where you will meet, and why their presence is valuable. You must help everyone understand that they are an essential part of moving your organization to greater success.

Make it fun.

Even if you have serious business to discuss, including some elements of fun or creativity will help keep everyone engaged and energized. Make it memorable. You should get people outside of their comfort zones, but be careful to structure activities that don't embarrass or single out someone for ridicule. You want to lift up every single person.

If this is the start of a major new initiative, consider shooting video of the meeting. Later, you can use pieces of the footage in a launch video and other employee communications.

Bring in a facilitator.

If you want honest feedback and idea generation, someone else should lead the conversation. A facilitator can get input that you can't because he's not the boss. Work ahead of time with your facilitator to define objectives. Ask him to query participants well in advance to take the temperature of the group so he's not going in cold.

Have a no-phone policy.

To get quality discussion and input, you need everyone to be mindful and fully present in the meeting. Phones should be packed away so people aren't distracted by buzzing, ringing, and social media temptations. Employees can let their outside contacts know ahead of time that they will be unavailable for a set amount of time, along with a backup plan for emergencies. Then put away the phones.

Feed their senses.

Offer delicious food and comfortable surroundings. Try to meet offsite. Think about all five senses and how to cater to them so the energy stays positive and proactive. Consider some breakouts with chair massages, music, and a "cool factor." Offer regular breaks with healthy snacks, and pay attention to when you might need to insert a time out.

Follow through.

At the meeting, the facilitator should recap discussion and establish future action steps and deadlines. Ideally, all participants should have some important assignments afterward. Then it's up to you to support your team. Fulfill your promises, and watch morale continue to grow, as ideas become real.

Having an effective retreat doesn't have to be like pulling teeth. Reinvigorate, refresh, and grow healthy new ideas with a better event.

MAKE YOUR EMPLOYEE-APPRECIATION EVENT ONE YOUR EMPLOYEES WILL ACTUALLY APPRECIATE

Employee-appreciation events are usually born of good intentions. But somewhere in the planning process, committees and "HAVE TOs" suck out all the fun faster than a Dyson Ball. Here are four ways to make your event a rousing success.

1. Say thank you and mean it.

At an employee event we coordinated recently, the CEO went to the front of the room and made a heartfelt thanks to the employees for all their work on achieving a major milestone. She reinforced her thanks by speaking about the mission and purpose of the organization—and made sure all the employees knew of their critical role in the work they do together.

During the informal times of the event, she mingled throughout the crowd to speak individually to employees and thank them one-on-one. All the employees left that event knowing they were valued and appreciated.

Saying thank you doesn't cost anything—and it speaks volumes.

2. Make it easy for your employees to attend.

The lunch event just referenced was a come-and-go format spread over a few hours that allowed employees to attend at a time that worked best in their work day and keep customers well served. Though it meant that the CEO was away from her office for an extended period, the flexibility showed that she respected employees' schedules.

A different organization who held an evening event provided child care at the party site. Those with young children didn't have the hassle or expense of hiring a babysitter. It meant that attending the event wasn't a hardship on the young parents, but, instead, a nice evening out. The positive feedback on this small touch was overwhelmingly positive.

3. Make the event mission-centered.

You should have a meaningful mission linked to your work. Use the employee appreciation event to underscore that.

What's your brand about?

- If your brand is about fun, be sure the event is fun for employees, too.

- If your brand is about financial health, make sure that

your event isn't at odds with what you promote and sell.

- If your mission is innovation, bring in some unique touches that allow creativity or new exploration.

4. Make the event thoughtful.

Leave the hams back in the '70s. Employee gifts should be something that people will really welcome and enjoy. Remember: it's about them, not about you.

Branded company swag will be welcome if it's high quality and well chosen. You can also offer gift cards and cash prizes. Even in small amounts, they're nice extras.

Consider creating some awards with unique names that reflect your culture. One organization we know presents "Sparky Awards" at its annual meeting. They're merely an announcement (no special plaque). But the praise is so cleverly written and presented for each honoree at this meeting that those who get a Sparky are glowing long after the event is over. A trophy is wonderful, but it may not be necessary if the recognition is thoughtfully crafted and presented with some flourish and razzle-dazzle.

> Wow them at your event so, next time around, all of them will be clamoring to RSVP... and even happier that they're a part of your organization.

Don't Wait

Whether you're considering a year-end annual meeting, a holiday party, or something else to thank employees, start thinking now. A memorable, well-branded employee event takes time. Devote careful attention to creating something people will look forward to eagerly, instead of hoping to merely make an appearance then sheepishly tiptoe out.

SWEET SIXTEEN: A CHECKLIST OF BEST PRACTICES FOR EVERY PROFITABLE BANK

Whether it's a new year, a midyear, or an end-of-year, it's always a good time to monitor your progress. Don't let this year's goals slip away because you were busy.

Here are sixteen strategies for a stronger, more profitable brand:

Nearly half of these best-brand practices involve employees. With their partnership and unwavering commitment to growing your organization, you'll thrive. Without them, the journey is ever so much harder.

1. Review and write down your successes from last year (not just financial ones but those in all areas of the bank).

2. Share them with your employees.

3. Find some unique, meaningful ways to thank employees—not once, but often.

4. Remember to celebrate.

5. Review/renew your plan and purpose.

6. Share it with your employees (bonus points if employees help review/renew).

7. Set some big, hairy audacious goals.

8. Break down the goals into bite-size pieces.

9. Be sure you're committed to the plan and purpose.

10. Ask employees to help the organization get there.

11. Set milestone markers of success.

12. Monitor and celebrate OR monitor and recalibrate.

13. Ask employees for ideas on purpose-centered ways to thank suppliers and referral sources.

14. Look for silos in your bank and build the necessary bridges that link employees and departments.

15. Ask employees for ideas on meaningful ways to thank customers and colleagues.

16. Repeat 1–15.

Don't forget to set benchmarks and to celebrate when you reach them. Or recalibrate when you don't.

STOP CALLING ON THE USUAL SUSPECTS FOR YOUR ADVISORY BOARD

Many of the community banks we've met have an advisory board of eight-to-ten local movers and shakers. Some of these boards have a diverse representation. Unfortunately, many are filled with the usual suspects. If you want your bank to stand the test of time, you must attract and retain the next generation of movers and shakers. That means you need diversity on your board.

Which target audiences are eluding you?

Lots of community bankers are scratching their heads about how to attract and retain young professionals. While FinTech offerings are a way to be sure you have the right product mix for up-and-coming people, that's not enough. More of your competitors are adding these products every day. That's not a differentiator; it's an expectation.

1. Go get the millennials.

Be bold. Don't just add one or two millennials to your existing board (though that might be a start). Go all in. Create a separate advisory board so you can center specific conversations on younger peoples' needs and concerns. Then, a few times a year, have both boards meet together.

Recruiting is easy.

- Reach out through your local chamber of commerce and civic organizations to spot the people who are leaders and influencers.

- Ask your young CSRs and other bankers to nominate some of their peers.

- Work with a local university to recruit a few of their top-notch seniors in business and entrepreneurship programs.

Tailor it to them.

- Expect to pay an honorarium.

- Meet at a time convenient to them (don't assume they're free for lunch or during business hours).

- Ask questions and be ready to listen, even when what they have to say stings a bit.

- Make a big deal of it: share their recruitment to your board through PR, social media, customer communications, their alumni publications, and your website.

2. Invite women and people of color.

Whether you're thinking about multiple advisory boards, or one blended board, age isn't the only consideration. You also need people of different backgrounds and experiences to help you see things you can't see on your own.

Recruiting is easy.

- Research your own customer base: who are some successful women or minority business owners who can bring value to your advisory team?

- Reach out through your local chamber of commerce and civic organizations to spot the people who are leaders and influencers.

- Look in the news: who are thought leaders doing notable work in volunteer and business circles?

Tailor it to them.

- Expect to pay an honorarium.

- Ask questions and be ready to listen, even when what they have to say stings a bit.

- Make a big deal of it: share their recruitment to your board through PR, social media, customer communications, their alumni publications, and your website.

Get busy.

Once you have input, develop ways to test and to put into action the ideas they have. Your job is to listen, to act, and to report back. It will be the beginning of some beautiful friendships.

WHAT'S GREEN AND GOES ROUND AND ROUND ALL DAY?

Your first answer might conjure playground riddles from first grade: a frog in a blender. But it also might be the answer to a common struggle for merging institutions: their advisory boards.

Without proper planning and an intentional effort, blending cultures of two advisory boards may cause things to "go round all day."

Trying to innovate or to create new solutions coming from entirely different foundations and frames of reference may bring about some real headaches. Here's how to avoid them.

The purpose of your advisory board.

While an advisory board isn't typically a policy-making body, it does serve vital functions. Its members help grow the institution through influence and advocacy. An effective advisory board does four things:

- Its members' ears are to the ground: they can let you know of changes in the community—or to your reputation—before you otherwise hear of them.

- They are opening doors for you: helping a business-development person get a meeting because they put in a good word for you is invaluable.

- They are banking with you: they can give honest feedback about products and services that you currently offer—or should be offering.

- They are your advocates in the community and in their spheres of influence. This is especially important in the case of a merger, because they can reassure and help set the record straight if there is any misinformation floating about.

The recipe.

The advisory board members are your insiders, so be sure you're treating them as trusted partners, not as an afterthought. Be sure you're taking these steps before the brand and the messaging are unveiled to the public.

Have a retreat.

Get all of them together, away from their everyday business, to focus on this work. Plan far enough ahead so that no one misses out. Use a facilitator to ensure that the conversation and activities are engaging and effective.

Share the vision.

Present the vision and mission of the newly blended institution. The advisory board members need to know what's changed and what's staying the same. In either case, articulate the WHYs and the HOWs that affect them, the employees, and the customers.

Ask for input.

Give the members time to listen to, to absorb, and to consider what they've heard. Ask for their questions. Allow them to poke holes into your messaging and your rationale. You've been working on this for a long time, and you're very close to it. They may bring up matters you've completely overlooked. Let them help you prepare to put your best foot forward when you unveil your new institution to the public.

Mix business and fun.

Help the members get to know each other. Moving forward, this group is going to need to work together. Create opportunities for socializing and fun so that if they don't already know one another, they have the opportunity to begin building some new relationships.

Not only does this recipe benefit your need for a cohesive board; it also benefits its members. They may begin to establish some ways they can work together or recommend each other in ways that benefit their businesses. That's win-win.

What the advisory board members need:

Talking Points

When the time is right, they need to be able to easily share the news correctly and on message. Give them a brief that illustrates key points about the benefits of your merger and how it benefits customers, suppliers, and the community.

Business Cards

One institution we've worked with provides business cards to its directors. Cards note the director's name and his or her position on the board, along with two contacts at the bank. This makes it easy for directors to make a referral at a business mixer or cocktail party.

That's an inexpensive way to keep your institution "out and about," with the added third-party endorsement of a director.

Updated Job Description and Paperwork

When you first recruited the directors, you probably gave them a job description, term limits, and an NDA. Is the compensation the same? Was it different for the two boards? If you haven't updated these things, the time is now. Be sure everyone has the same expectations, and you won't be tripped up because of an oversight.

Shout-Outs

Be sure to send out news releases highlighting the advisory directors of your newly combined institution. Post them on your website and in your customer communications. The positive press will make the directors feel good. It will also give you another PR hit that brings more visibility about your bank, its purpose, and the stellar people on your board.

Set the tone for a perfectly blended, fully functioning board of advocates that shapes your institution's future. Plan properly for your newly blended advisory board, and you'll crush it.

BLENDING CULTURES IN A MERGER: THREE LESSONS FROM *THE BRADY BUNCH*

Mergers and acquisitions are increasingly commonplace in the financial industry. So if your institution is joining or acquiring another, what do you do to ensure a perfectly blended culture that leads to consistent brand and customer experience at all branches? Your employer brand is at stake, so where can you turn?

Look no further than the '70s-era TV show, *The Brady Bunch*, for inspiration. Here are three takeaways you can use to get started.

Make sure that the only "steps" lead to the second floor.

Recognize that, at first, there will be some awkward adjustments, as people try to figure out how they fit into the new organization. Who's the new boss? What are my expectations? Questions will be many. Anxiety may rise.

In an early episode, Mom/Carol told Bobby that the only "steps" in their household led to the second floor. Her point: that the family contains no "stepchildren," only "children."

Set the expectation that all are important and have something valuable to contribute in the new institution, no matter where they started. Then clearly articulate their new roles in the new structure. Communicate, communicate, and communicate some more. Help all feel like part of the team.

And, just as important, expect them to treat others as teammates, not rivals.

Be sure you have an Alice.

Someone has to be the bridge. You need an Alice who connects everyone. In the Brady family, the housekeeper was often the neutral party who helped improve communications with a batch of cookies, a listening ear, and some wisdom sprinkled with humor. Someone in the role of Chief Heart Officer can make sure that your brand, purpose, and people values are never overlooked, while you're working on implementing the new systems, software, and procedures that are also so critical.

You don't want a mass exodus of employees because of discontent and mistrust. That leads to dissatisfied customers, as well. A proactive approach is always best. And if problems do arise, you've got someone ready to quickly address them.

Create a catchy theme song.

Perhaps you don't need a song, literally. But then again, it might set just the right tone. Or maybe it's an internal launch party with a video, break room posters, social media, retreats, or other attention-getting events. This isn't just black-and-white: bring in the emotion. What do you want to convey? Whether it's pride, patriotism, teamwork, adventure, overcoming the odds, or something else, invite people in so that they genuinely feel part of your purpose.

Whatever the approach, if you inform and inspire while sharing what you want to accomplish, you'll go further—faster.

An intentional and well-planned approach to building culture through shared activities and values building will help everyone thrive. The song—and other creative strategies— bring the emotion and the rallying cry that brings people together.

Whether your blended institution is old-school, like *The Brady Bunch*, or more like *Modern Family*, it takes real effort to make your approach work. The three lessons above are just a starting point. While you're planning the functional details, be sure you're working out the culture details, too. They are just as important. Don't let them be an afterthought, or customers and employees will feel the pain. You will, too.

EXPERIENCE LIVES ON LONG AFTER THE SALE

"Our brands—Nike, Converse, Jordan Brand and Hurley—are loved by customers all over the world. But we never take that for granted; we know that every day we have to earn their trust—by serving them completely and adding real value to their lives through products and experiences."
—MARK PARKER, CEO OF NIKE

"Customer loyalty comes from consistent experience. They learn to count on you."
—JIMMY JOHN LIAUTAUD, FOUNDER AND CHAIRMAN OF JIMMY JOHN'S SANDWICH CHAIN

"You have to create a consistent brand experience however and wherever a customer touches your brand, online or offline. The lines are forever blurred."
—ANGELA AHRENDTS, FORMER CEO AT BURBERRY AND SENIOR VICE PRESIDENT OF RETAIL SERVICES AT APPLE

ANYONE CAN GIVE CUSTOMER SERVICE: EXPERIENCES SERVE YOUR BANK BETTER

Stellar customer experience outdistances customer service every time.

Experience is the feeling captured from something that happened that made you feel really good—or really bad. It conjures emotion, and it sticks with you. That feeling outlives the minor frustrations, the minor delights, or the things that merely go "right."

The image lives on because you made it notable. In their book, *The Power of Moments*, Chip Heath and Dan Heath tell how certain brief experiences can make an enormous difference in peoples' lives—and how we must create these extraordinary moments in our life and work.

When you plan creatively, you can create powerful, memorable experiences for employees and customers.

Make your experiences so remarkable that it's hard for them to see themselves going anywhere else.

CUSTOMER EXPERIENCE CHECKLIST

The basics first.

On the phone
- How long does a customer wait on hold?
- What is your on-hold message or music?
- What does your voice mail actually say, and is it branded?
- If you left a message, did you get a return call within the same business day?

In the bank
- Is the environment inviting?

- How does it smell?
- How long does a customer wait before being acknowledged?
- Does the banker use the customer's name?
- Does the customer observe teamwork or strife between bankers?
- Does the customer feel his presence is an interruption of the conversation of two bankers?
- If the banker needs to take the customer to another department, does she make an introduction?
- Are desks clean and clutter-free?
- Is the lobby clean and well-organized?
- Are the restrooms clean and stocked?
- Is the customer bar area clean and stocked with pens and necessary supplies?
- Are the bankers wearing name tags?
- Are the bankers professionally dressed?
- Do the signs and posters look bright and unfaded, and professionally hung?
- Is there an appropriate area for customers to manage their safe deposit boxes in privacy and comfort?

Online and apps
- Does the online banking work in any browser?
- Is it simple to sign up?
- Is it easy to navigate and get what you want?
- Is the app easy to use?
- Are there annoying pop-ups users have to work around?

ATM
- Is is stocked with supplies?
- Is it clean?
- Is it well-lit?

- Does it feel safe to use after dark?

Drive-through

- Is the window clean or smudgy?
- Is the work area professional and organized?
- Is the wait time appropriate?
- Does the deposit tube have an extra pen?
- Is the pen bank-branded?
- Is the tube clean?
- Are the notices posted at the window fresh and professional?
- Is the driveway clear of debris?

Even better are the experience extras.

To be a standout bank and build the relationships that really last, you must create memories. Here are some idea starters to get you thinking about the ways you could elevate your institution and take it from a service institution to an experience institution.

You have access to important customer milestones; do you act on them?

You know when your customers are having some of the most momentous events in their lives: new job, baby, new home, planning for a wedding, going to college, surviving the death of a spouse. Do you recognize these events and share your warmest wishes with them?

- You know a customer's birthday. Do you send a card?

- You know a customer's business anniversary. Do you send a card or post a social media shout-out?

- What kinds of surprises could you offer from out of the blue?

One bank we know dresses up one-dollar bills with stick-on rabbit faces at Easter time. Then the bankers go around town, dropping in at customer businesses and handing out "Bunny Bucks." It's a welcome surprise that costs them very little, but it makes a big impact.

Another institution we know has bankers clean customer windshields at the drive-through. What if that bank also held monthly carwash fund-raisers on behalf of their nonprofit clients?

I would love an antigerm towelette at drive-throughs during flu and cold season.

How about a fresh cookie or a chocolate handed out with my receipt?

You're already snapping your customers' photos at the drive-up: can you make the photos fun "selfies" to share with them?

What if you sent Valentine's cards for no other reason than to show appreciation?

Could you use your marquee to share customer and employee shout-outs?

What if you scheduled a behind-the-scenes "show-and-tell" of the vault- and safe-deposit-box areas to customers' children?

What could you do that's memorable?

WHAT THE GIRL SCOUTS CAN TEACH BANKERS ABOUT CUSTOMER EXPERIENCE

Soon, Girl Scout Cookie time will return. Over the years, you've come to expect—and thoroughly enjoy—your purchase experience. Whether your favorite is Thin Mints or

Samoas, you might think the cookies are a little pricey. And you also think they're worth every indulgent bite.

So what do the Girl Scouts have to teach bankers about customer experience? Everything.

The customers at your institution should have a consistent experience online, at ATMs, and in person at every branch. The Girl Scouts have a guide. Do you?

Girl Scouts don't just "make it up." When they're selling their wares, they know:

The presentation

They're taught the proper polite and friendly greeting, how to navigate the order form competently, what to wear, and how to be confident in what they ask. You have probably noticed their sashes with the badges they've earned. If you were in scouting, those badges probably summon some memories of your own accomplishments. Awwww!

The details

They know the insides and outs of price, the quantity per box, which are gluten free or vegan, and when those addictive treats will deliver.

The "why"

They are not just selling cookies. They can tell you about how your purchase is supporting camp, girl empowerment, and the teaching of entrepreneurship. They will impress you with their stories. In other words, they are firm in their purpose and mission—and it shows.

The process

They know the step-by-step process, the reporting, and the best ways to communicate with each other. Because it's institutionalized, the process works seamlessly for volunteers and customers.

The roles and responsibilities

Girl Scouts have a strong hierarchy—with cookie chairs, leaders, and girls all working together in their respective roles. They all support and help one another up and down the chain.

Experience trumps service every time.

Isolated "great-service" events will only get you so far. Awe-inspiring customer service and true brand loyalty start with a consciously designed customer experience that's consistent and memorable at every brand touch point.

DO NOT WRITE MY NAME ON MY CLOTHES— AND OTHER THINGS YOU DO FOR YOUR CONVENIENCE INSTEAD OF MINE

It's been a while, but I'm still fuming about the dry cleaner who wrote my name inside my clothes. With a Sharpie. Really!? This isn't summer camp, and I'm not eight years old.

While this happened months ago, I'm still dismayed.

I get it. They were trying to do a good job—to avoid mixing up peoples' garments—they thought the indelible ink was a brilliant idea. The problem is that it's only a good idea for them. Now when I take the blouse off the hanger, I see that mess on my nice, designer-label, and it bothers me.

It's gotten me thinking about how many other places and times customers put up with something that's easy for the business but not easy or pleasant for the one paying the bill.

Financial institutions can be especially guilty. Here are some examples:

- The account statements with cryptic descriptions of charges and transactions. (Honestly, what regular person knows these terms?)

- The online banking portal that works only in one browser.

- The ATM that's sometimes stocked with supplies, but not always.

- The automated phone system that takes the caller through nine levels of Hades before getting to a real person.

I also know some stellar bankers. I'll give a big shout-out to my treasury management consultant, who gave me her cell number and actually answers it on the weekends (that's putting customers first). I deeply appreciate her, and I promise not to take advantage of her. I am loyal.

No one's perfect. As a leader at your institution, you must be constantly on the lookout for ways to endear your customers to your brand. Before you give them a logoed water bottle, be sure you're making their user experience the best ever.

Bankers: have you secret-shopped your institution? If not, do it now.

PARDON ME, BUT YOUR SLIP IS SHOWING

An occasional slipup can make your brand look bruised. More than one can make it smell rotten. Your competitors may find it as entertaining as a Marx Brothers sketch. You won't.

Here are some trouble spots to look out for—and what to do about them.

Your employee reminders are sending the wrong messages (to the wrong people).

Many financial institutions have signage tucked behind the teller line reminding bankers to suggest more products or pitch a new promotion. Some are even handwritten, unpolished documents on sticky notes or scrap paper.

These send messages you don't want:

- When I come through the drive-through for an in-person transaction, I can see those notes behind the counter. They're hidden to walk-up traffic but not to drivers like me. They tell me you're just trying to *sell* me, not *help* me.

- Employees seeing hastily scrawled or unprofessional-looking notes see something else: they see something that isn't really that important, because little care and attention has been placed on communicating this initiative with them. Don't be surprised when they don't recommend another product to me.

You think employees can read your mind.

Lots of CEOs believe employees should be suggesting, counseling, selling. Leaders sometimes don't understand why employees aren't making this a priority. But do employees know this is the expectation?

Be sure you're communicating your expectations and the business plan clearly and regularly.

- Do you have a written protocol for consultative selling?

- Do employees have the customer data at their fingertips to help them suggest the right kinds of products to the customer standing in front of them?

- Are employees trained or just handed the book and told to do it?

- Are employees hired, reminded, and evaluated on the basis of your expectations?

If not, chances are that you're frustrated—and they are, too. Sales and new relationships will slide. Not because of bad service, but because of bad training.

Your physical plant looks wilted and tired.

You're saving money and returning more dividends to shareholders. Efficiency is important, but if it looks as if no one is minding the shop, it sends a signal that your brand isn't prosperous. No one wants that from her financial institution. Don't be penny-wise and pound-foolish. Take a look at:

- Signage: is it bright and fresh or faded by the sunlight?

- Parking lot and drive-up: are they clean, well-lit, and free of trash, snow, or other obstacles?

- Lobby decor: are the chairs threadbare? Get rid of the dusty artificial plants. Right now.

- ATM: is it clean, unfaded, and well-stocked with supplies?

Ensure that the brick-and-mortar expression of your brand is well-kept. That tells customers their finances are also well-kept.

Secret-shop yourself.

Even the best-tended brands can slip up on occasion. Take some time out now to evaluate your performance. Be sure you're communicating in a way that's on par with your brand—for employees *and* customers.

WHAT TOURIST-Y RESTAURANTS CAN TEACH BANKERS ABOUT BEING STICKY

I was a tourist in Branson, Missouri, recently, and, as to be expected, I had some subpar experiences in the crowded restaurants. Many eateries seemed perfectly happy offering mediocre food and sticky seats. They know I probably won't be back, because some other stranger will take my place. They're just in it for today's dollar.

On the flip side, you actually want stickiness in your institution. You're in it for today's and tomorrow's dollars.

Here's what you can learn from a restaurant with the right kind of sticky.

Welcome.

Landry's stood head and shoulders above the rest, because every touch point was consistently, exceedingly good. They were there to give me a customized experience. Unlike most others on the strip, they had thought of everything. We arrived weary and early for our reservation, so we went to the lounge for a cool drink. The bartender introduced herself. She went through some mental gymnastics to get us the best appetizer combo. She asked if we were locals or visitors, and she made us feel welcome.

They knew our names.

When our reservation time came up, we were seated promptly. We received personalized menus with a welcome message and our names at the top. Remarkable. Fun.

When we sat down, the server already knew our names. Can I repeat that? *The server knew our names.* She greeted us warmly, and remembered each of us the whole evening. And we weren't her only table.

They made us feel smart.

The server (Mary—I remember her, too) obviously knew the products and the wine. She asked what we liked, and she usually affirmed our choices with a nod or a few words like, "That's a really good choice," or, "I think you'll like that." (Have you ever noticed how that makes you feel?)

They knew their brand.

All of them there knew their stuff. They were proud to be working there. They were professional: from their uniforms, to their attitude, to their product knowledge. They all were an excellent representation of the brand. They had hit a home run. No, a grand slam. Was it expensive? Yes. Did it hurt? No. We received an incredible amount of value.

Four DOs that apply to your financial institution:

DO anticipate the customers' needs. Don't be content to be merely an order-taking banker. Know what your customer and her business is doing. Read the trades. Follow her company on social media. Listen. That way, you can ask intelligent questions and offer appealing recommendations.

DO affirm your customers' choices. Once you've listened and guided, reassure them so they feel great about the (much more) important decisions you're helping them make.

DO wear your name tag so customers and prospects learn your name. Make it easy and pleasurable to do business with you. Be memorable and be referable.

DO have customer names already filled in on paperwork. Like the customized menus, it's a nice surprise. It also saves time for the customer and for you.

Don't be like the hordes of restaurants and attractions who treat people with a devil-may-care attitude. Just because it's painful for customers to leave you doesn't mean they won't. If they're neglected, they will tell others. Eventually, no matter how many products they have with you, they'll take their hard-earned dollars elsewhere.

WHAT DALE CARNEGIE AND BEYONCÉ TEACH US ABOUT RELATIONSHIPS

Almost all community banks will boast that they know their customers by their names. But do you really?

And do you teach your bankers to go further than just recognizing familiar faces and saying customers' names out loud? It might be a little old school, but it will be music to their ears.

Rule #6.

Dale Carnegie's Rule #6—published in 1936—is *"Remember that a person's name is to that person the sweetest and most important sound in any language."* It's true. When your bankers are talking to a customer, a supplier, or each other, using their names builds bridges.

"Uh-huh" and "yeah, okay."

Beyoncé knows it, too. In 1999, Destiny's Child reinforced what Dale told us long ago. *"You're acting kinda shady. Every other word is 'uh-huh, yeah, okay.'"* The mega hit was "Say My Name."

Beyoncé and Dale have a lot in common. They understood

the power of a name.

My name means everything. Uh-huh means nothing.

It's never old school to make someone feel good.

You make individuals feel noticed, included, and valued when you say their names. Here are three easy ways to do just that:

1. When they arrive for an appointment: it's easy to look at the calendar and find the visitor's name. Your greeter should say "Hello, Julie! I'll let Patrick know you're here." It's easy as apple pie.

2. When they call on the phone: they've probably identified themselves already. Teach your bankers to write that name down immediately. Then repeat it back. "Thank you for calling, Julie. I'll transfer you immediately." Bonus points for wrapping up with a branded message.

3. When they visit a branch: train your bankers to use the technology in front of their eyes. When they're conducting a transaction, it's easy to know who's in front of them. Even if they can't recall her name when she walks up, by the middle of your conversation they should know. They can take advantage of the opportunity to say, "I appreciate you taking the time to stop by, Julie. What else can we do for you while you're here?"

Though it may seem old school, saying customers' names aloud is an endearing—and often underused—habit to have in this hurried, modern world. It will make all the difference between a transaction and a relationship.

HOW A HOUND DOG AND A HANDSHAKE BRED ENDURING LOYALTY

My ninety-three-year-old father-in-law, Ralph, is a World War II veteran and a serial entrepreneur. Over the years, he's owned a night club, a dry cleaning shop, a demolition business, and more. He's an excellent negotiator, and he knows how to lead and inspire a team.

And he knows firsthand the value of a strong banking relationship.

Ralph loves to tell a story about how, one weekend many years ago, he bought $2,100 worth of antiques at an auction, with plans to resell them at a profit. When he bought the antiques, he didn't have the money to cover the check he had written. So, on Monday morning, he called his banker to tell him what he'd done and ask for a loan to cover the check.

The banker asked what collateral he had. "Well, I've got an old hound dog," Ralph said.

"I guess that will be enough," said the banker. And the deal was done.

Though lenders of today—and our regulator friends— would frown on such a deal, the lesson is powerful.

Their relationship lasted many years.

His banker was trusted, tried, and true.

Though you can't do a deal over a handshake and a hound dog today, you can look for ways to help your customers— both large and small—succeed in their businesses. As a lender, you should be a counselor and a valued teammate. Are you there when they're in a pinch? Do you help them look ahead?

Are you asking the right questions to serve in that role?

- What type of loan structure best suits his business?

- Would it be better for her to buy or lease that major equipment?

- How are the tax changes affecting his ability to grow?

- What working capital does she need to get to the next level?

If you ask and advise, you're no commodity. You're a go-to. When your customers are profitable and prosperous, your institution is, too. You'll create enduring loyalty that becomes legendary.

THREE THINGS EVERY BANKER CAN DO BETTER: LESSONS FROM IKEA

Do you think IKEA is just about low-cost furniture for dorms? Think again. It's a company well-founded in purpose, offering "nesting" and affordable design for all. IKEA can teach every

Welcome

banker how to grow loyalty and profit from the inside out.

Here are three important ways:

1. Lead customers through your "store."

At IKEA, there's a prescribed path from the entrance to the check out. IKEA wants to be sure its shoppers know about everything it has to offer—not merely what they came to shop for—so it leads customers through the store with illuminated arrows on the floor. It also posts maps in multiple places so shoppers can find what they want.

While I don't propose that you force people to walk through your bank along a certain route, you should ask yourself whether customers really know everything you have to offer them.

What about online? Are you leading them to what they want—and what they might need? Are you making it easy or frustrating?

If they are not fully banked with you, do you know why? Have your customers been lured to doing business with other institutions that have done a better job assessing their needs? Or do they simply have financial needs going unmet?

Either way, you must *lead* and *educate* so that customers get what they need, not just what they came to buy.

2. Treat customers like family and friends.

IKEA customers can sign up to be part of its "family" for free. Once signed up, they receive discounts, free in-store child care, complimentary coffee and tea in the cafe, and other in-store benefits.

Besides the in-store perks, IKEA also gives families buy-one-get-one tickets to museums and attractions located nearby.

Friends bring friends. IKEA recognizes that, too, and it offers easy ways for its "family" members to bring their friends into the fold.

Many banks don't offer loyalty programs. Some have loyalty programs that don't offer the benefits customers really appreciate and use. Others have nice benefits—but only if customers jump through a ton of hoops.

- A bank that encourages financial responsibility should offer programs for kids and seminars for adults that support those values.

- An institution focusing on small businesses could partner with the local SBA to provide support on financial management, taxes, DBE certifications, and other issues.

Follow IKEA's lead. Make your program easy, and be sure it fits your brand attributes.

3. Treat employees like customers.

IKEA wears its heart on its sleeve. The employment page displays its values loud and clear. You'll see attributes like:

- Leadership by example
- Togetherness and enthusiasm
- Humbleness and willpower
- Simplicity
- Cost-consciousness
- Striving to meet reality
- Constant desire for renewal
- Constantly being "on the way"

What's really notable about IKEA's values? They're not the run-of-the-mill values seen on corporate walls everywhere. They're genuine and inspiring.

On IKEA's website, you'll see store associates giving testimonials and talking about their growth opportunities with the company.

Are you showing prospective employees your true brand—or bland?

Take a look at your institution's employment page. If it sounds something like this, you're like almost everyone else—and not very attractive:

We offer competitive salaries, flexible hours, great benefits, and the opportunity for advancement in both full- and part-time employment. No financial experience is needed—just a big smile and the drive to be part of our team!

ICK.

IKEA has won renown as a top innovative company numerous times. IKEA knows that happy employees are more effective and sell more.

Make it a whole experience.

IKEA delivers an entire experience at every brand touch point. Customers know what it offers, are loyal, and bring their friends. Those same attributes can drive your institution's business forward as well.

HOW TO AVOID A ZOMBIE BRAND-POCALYPSE

Zombies have much in common with angry current and former employees. They can decimate a brand as quickly as a village in your favorite horror movie.

Watch for the warning signs or it may be too late.

There are three main characteristics.

According to the Zombie Research Society, zombies have three main characteristics: 1) they are reanimated corpses, 2) they are relentlessly aggressive, and 3) they are infected and infectious.

1. Reanimated corpses

You may have them—and now you'll recognize them immediately. They might be employees who are:

- Weary and numb; they haven't had a good coach or mentor to help them grow.

- Burned out and unengaged with your vision.

- Overworked, with no help in sight.

- The grumblers who never shared your purpose but just want a paycheck.

They are literally dead on their feet. They may be stumbling, bumping into things, and groaning aloud. It can be terrifying to other employees and customers, who must flee for cover.

2. Relentlessly aggressive

Zombies never quit. In their relentless pursuit of brains, they're almost unstoppable.

Make sure to give your employees food for their own brains so they're not getting starved out.

- Are staff meetings and working environment steeped in your culture?

- Do you regularly share the business goals and progress toward reaching them?

- Are training budgets adequate to support your employees' personal growth and innovative ideas?

- Do employees have the tools and the latitude they need to deliver upon your brand promise?

If you're not feeding them, they'll hungrily search for another position—and kill your brand's reputation, as they spew out their venom on anyone who will listen. They can be lethal.

3. Infected—and infectious

The zombies in most movies create more of their kind with a bite. In your organization, the bite could show up as rumor mongering, playing politics, or troublemaking that gets other people riled up. It can spread like pinkeye at a day care.

Employees who were previously ambivalent will "turn." Good employees will adopt bunker mentality, as they fight for their lives. Soon, you have an epidemic.

Don't tolerate bad actors. Inoculate your employees and protect your brand by taking swift action.

Be vigilant.

Watch for the telltale signs: employees just going through the motions or doing the minimum to get by and loyal customers and employees suddenly going missing.

If any one employee has all three of these issues, he may be past saving. If you have many employees with these issues, it could take radical action to save your brand. And remember to double-tap.

SIXTEEN WAYS TO MAKE COMMERCIAL CUSTOMERS FEEL LIKE ROCK STARS

Are you making yourself indispensable to your business customers? Treat them like rock stars, and they'll have little reason to consider doing business with any other institutions. You don't have to stock their offices with M&M's (minus a certain color) and a gourmet brand of sparkling water.

You do need to treat them as if they're special, because they are.

Here are sixteen easy ways to give them the VIP treatment.

1. Invite them to special events at your bank—or out in the community.

2. Use your social media to give them shout-outs.

3. Follow their social media and comment/congratulate them on their achievements.

4. Be their customer, too.

5. Nominate them for awards in the community or in their industry.

6. Send them handwritten thank-you notes.

7. Introduce them to others who could become their prospects and customers.

8. Schedule a business review and help them maximize their finances.

9. Listen.

10. Set meetings at their place of business instead of yours.

11. Highlight them in your marketing.

12. Surprise their employees with a basket of treats.

13. Invite them to set up displays about their products or services in your lobby.

14. Offer a valuable educational lunch-and-learn to their employees.

15. Offer VIP-only extended hours for access to safety-deposit boxes or other needs.

16. Listen some more.

Take the time to focus on building your customers' success, and you'll build your own brand capital at the same time. Encore!

SIXTEEN WAYS TO MAKE RETAIL CUSTOMERS FEEL LIKE VIPS

Are you making yourself indispensable to your retail customers? Not only are they "regular people"; they may also be the business owners you're serving with different products or referral sources within their own networks.

Be sure you're making solid offerings to these customers who have different—yet also important—needs.

Show them how much they mean to you.

1. Invite them to special events at your bank or out in the community.

2. Follow their social media, and comment on the cute photos of their families, pets, and pet projects.

3. Make sure your digital-branch experience feels like a personal event, though it's online.

4. Nominate them for awards in the community.

5. Send them handwritten thank-you notes.

6. Create affinity groups to help them get to know each other—and your institution—better.

7. Schedule a yearly review to help them maximize their finances.

8. Ask for their feedback on improving your products and services through a survey or focus groups.

9. Listen.

10. Highlight them in your marketing.

11. Surprise them with something out of the ordinary at the drive-through.

12. Offer a valuable educational lunch-and-learn that helps them make better financial decisions.

13. Offer VIP-only extended hours for access to safety-deposit boxes or other needs.

14. Send birthday cards or holiday greetings other than at Christmas time.

15. Graciously forgive a mistake.

16. Listen some more.

YOU'RE NOT MAKING IT EASY FOR ME TO DO BUSINESS WITH YOU

Dear Community Banker X: Your technology is behind. Your ATM is dysfunctional, and you don't seem to care whether I can easily do business with you or not. I'm sending out an SOS.

You're a bank who advertises, who sponsors lots of local events, and who has employees at all the chamber of commerce meetings. Maybe you're wondering why your marketing isn't working as well as it used to.

It isn't the marketing that's the problem. It's something much deeper.

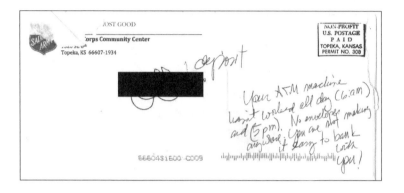

Here's a true story.

Two weeks ago, I needed to deposit a paper check at a local bank before it opened for the day. The ATM couldn't dispense an envelope, so I scrounged up an envelope at the bottom of my glove compartment, only to discover that the ATM couldn't accept my deposit at all. I came back after hours (about twelve hours later), and the bank was still unavailable to do business with me.

In frustration, I drove around to the archaic night-deposit drop. I stepped out of my car and slipped my envelope through the slot—after dark, which I really do not like—but not before I scrawled a note of frustration on the outside of the envelope.

Whoever opened for business the next day had to have seen my envelope, because my online banking shows the bank received the deposit. Did he or she not read my message?

This bank must not really care, because I haven't heard a word. And it's been two weeks. The bank had plenty of time to make it up to me.

Three things are terribly wrong about this story.
1) Employees haven't been trained to care or to act.
Boilerplate training manuals tell employees to smile, to call the customer by name, and to ask, "Is there anything else I can do for you today?" Employees make sure that there are cookies in the lobby and that there's some kind of coffee.

That kind of culture is fairly easy to produce.

What's harder—and even more important—is creating a culture of problem-solving employees. Those are the people who will take responsibility and who will treat the business as if they were the owners, rather than sweeping the frustrated message into the waste bin with an "it's not my job" attitude.

A high-performance brand has employees who take notice of the customers' signals of frustration. They reach out with a call and a solution.

Is this bank so inundated with frustrated customers that they can't possibly all be answered? If so, there are even bigger issues looming ahead.

2) Leaders know they're sticky, so they're lazy.
Every banker knows that once a customer is signed up for direct deposit paychecks, online banking, and automatic monthly payments, it's perceived as a huge hassle for that customer to leave.

This makes some banks lazy. They think it doesn't really matter: once they have the customer, he's a customer for life. That may be so.

But if that customer is dissatisfied, he'll never recommend that bank to a friend. And if he has new financial needs, I can almost guarantee he'll go to another financial institution that, incidentally, was recommended to him by someone else.

That means loss of repeat business, the extremely valuable word-of-mouth recommendation—and profit.

3) Owners haven't invested in the business.

Customers don't need a brick-and-mortar branch on every corner. Just as they have come to depend on Netflix and their DVR, they want their financial institutions to be available when they have the time to manage their finances. They expect technology that enables them to bank at their convenience. They also expect real people to help them when they call.

Owners must wisely invest in their businesses to be viable for the future. Those who put care into their brands, their employees, and their technology will come out on top.

I've been lazy, too—but not any longer.

How would your institution stand up to similar scrutiny? The cleverest advertising on the planet won't help, if you don't invest in the business of your institution.

I'm shopping for a new bank. I think I can manage the hassle that will get me to a relationship that is satisfying for both of us. Will you notice when I—and my money—are gone? Have a nice day.

I MAKE A MISTAKE; I PAY. YOU MAKE A MISTAKE; I PAY!?

I talk about banking with a lot of people. So, last month, someone told me about accidentally hitting "submit" on an

ACH transaction twice. Fortunately, a banker called right away to inquire about whether it was a duplicate and got it reversed. There was a $30+ charge for that fix, but it saved some money and hassle in the long run.

Now, compare that to an accident the bank made on this same company's credit card accounts.

There was a sizable mystery payment the company couldn't account for and had no record of making.

After much sleuthing, it was discovered that someone else's deposit had been mistakenly credited to my acquaintance's account. This was a big hassle for his staff—and most likely, the other business, who's also trying to figure out why their payment has gone missing.

Besides the *"gosh, we're sorry"* and *"we'll get it fixed soon,"* that was the end of it from the bank's perspective.

Some people are feeling shortchanged.

Mistakes like this at most institutions are few and far between. Sadly, when they do make a mistake, most borrow on laziness and think it's OK.

Set a new standard.

A bank we've consulted with developed a customer promise that if the bank made a mistake, it would pay a rebate to the customer. It was part of their "Banking UNusual" promise.

Unusual? Yes. Uncommon? Absolutely.

Don't be penny-wise and pound-foolish.

1. Make sure your employees know the appropriate way to respond to a customer concern. *"Gee, I'm sorry"* isn't

good enough. Trying to sweep it under the rug is bad form. Train employees to empathize and respond appropriately, in accordance with your policies.

2. Fix it fast. If you can't be the first to discover the error, at least address it with lightning speed.

3. If you make a mistake, emulate Nordstrom (or Banking UNusual). The payback you'll get from word of mouth both in real life and on social media will far exceed the $30 it cost you to reimburse the customer.

The competition is tougher than ever.

You know that competition isn't just across the street—it's across the globe. Don't let customers slip away because you're not giving them the local touch you say you're famous for.

THE SURPRISINGLY EFFECTIVE RESPONSE TO A CUSTOMER COMPLAINT

I recently had trouble with a community bank's technology and emailed a banker there to complain in what I hope was a polite—but very frustrated—manner. The response was swift and unexpected.

She thanked me.

The first part of the surprise.

Of course, she called to apologize. That's expected. But she also *thanked me,* saying she appreciated my bringing this issue to her attention so she could look into it and get it resolved. Her approach was brilliant, because she made me feel as if I were helping her.

The second part.

A few days later, I received a $50 gift certificate and a thank-you note in the mail from this banker. She took the time to write a note. She went further by including a gift.

She went far above and beyond the call of duty, and it WOWED me.

Be like her.

This is one smart banker. She didn't just work on solving the problem; she did much more.

Thanking a complainer is an unusual—and effective—tactic for two reasons:

1. While I may be the only one who complained, there are likely to be others who have had the same experience and are just as frustrated.

2. I'm telling all my friends about the sensational customer service I just received at this bank. That's powerful ROI for the promotional dollar.

See the opportunity.

A report published in 2019 by the American Bankers Association wrote that while customer satisfaction with the association's banks has improved, 20 percent of the customers are still dissatisfied. This means there's plenty of opportunity for you to grow market share. It also means many of your customers may be dissatisfied and thinking about switching financial institutions. So start listening and thanking right now.

You're welcome.

"NOT A PROBLEM" IS FOR LAZY BRANDS

"Not a problem," the CSR said to me on the phone, as we were wrapping up my transaction. What!? Not a problem? For who—you!? Wait a minute. Who is the customer here?

All too often, the tellers, the sales clerks, and the recruiters think they're being polite when they respond to my "thank-you" with "not a problem." You may not be surprised by it in a fast food joint. Yet it can be heard almost anywhere.

I don't blame the employees. I blame you.

"Not a problem" is passive. And it's lazy. You want a culture of proactive people who are aligned with your purpose to solve a customer's need. Here are three ways to shore up your brand from the inside out:

1. Train

Employees should be trained and positioned as counselors, advisors, and experts.

When they have that competence (and confidence), they can easily listen, then suggest what a customer needs. Rather than simply acting as order takers who say goodbye with ambivalence, they can sell more, while, at the same time, giving customers what they actually need.

2. Model

How are you acting? What is your language? Do you say "not a problem" to internal customers? Or do you listen, counsel, and support?

And even if you don't actually say it, do you project "not a problem" by failing to give people your full attention when they're meeting with you? If they're getting a glassy-eyed response from you, it's almost the same thing. Be courteous and mindful.

3. Reward

Be sure you're reporting back to employees about the difference they're making. Reward them with praise and bonuses. You'll create a circle of reciprocity that benefits everyone.

Banish "not a problem" from your institution's vocabulary.

It may seem like a subtle change, but it conveys a completely different kind of attitude.

YOU, MY FRIEND, ARE IN SALES

"I have always said that everyone is in sales. Maybe you don't hold the title of salesperson, but if the business you are in requires you to deal with people, you, my friend, are in sales."
—ZIG ZIGLAR, AMERICAN AUTHOR, SALESMAN, AND MOTIVATIONAL SPEAKER

"Really good customer service will deliver sales. You are training salesmen to give the best possible advice and then to achieve the sale. People actually like you to ask for a sale because it shows you value their business."
—JOHN CAUDWELL, FOUNDER OF MOBILE PHONE RETAILER PHONES 4U

"To me, mentorships and internships are two big pillars in business development. I believe in having multiple mentors."
—TROY CARTER, FOUNDER, CHAIRMAN, AND CEO OF ATOM FACTORY

"Pretend that every single person you meet has a sign around his or her neck that says, 'Make me feel important.' Not only will you succeed in sales, you will succeed in life."
—MARY KAY ASH, FOUNDER OF MARY KAY COSMETICS

"To me, job titles don't matter. Everyone is in sales. It's the only way we stay in business."
—HARVEY MACKAY, BUSINESSMAN, AUTHOR, AND SYNDICATED COLUMNIST

BUSINESS DEVELOPMENT IS EVERYONE'S JOB

Sales gets a bad rap. And, often, the idea of cold calling strikes fear in the hearts of even the most seasoned bankers.

"Everyone should know how great we are," they tell themselves. Or they think of sales as "the loan officer's job." But you know that business development isn't only about loan revenue.

I hope you also know that while all might think you're really great, they probably think several other bankers—your competitors—are great, too.

So what does this mean? It means you must establish a mind-set all throughout your institution that:

1) Everyone is able to—and expected to—grow new and existing customer relationships.

2) Growing your loan portfolio is only one part of business development.

3) Loan officers do not sit by the phone, waiting for it to ring.

4) Business development happens inside the bank, and also

at the PTO, within civic groups, on social media, in faith communities, and everywhere else your staffers go.

5) Knowledgeable, cross-trained universal bankers are valued and rewarded.

While all may know how terrific your institution is, they still haven't all been invited to bank with you—or bank more with you. It's your job to set the tone, to educate, and to model the behavior that grows your business and your bottom line.

WHY YOUR OFFICER-CALLING PROGRAM IS DESTINED TO FAIL

You have new marketing brochures, a fantastic iPad sales presentation, and you're ready to turn your bankers loose. You're certain this is the time they'll get out there and land some shiny new relationships.

Will they do it? Or are you going to be disappointed again? Here are three reasons your campaign is destined to fail—and how to fix it.

1. You have an order-taking culture.

It's not just you. Most financial institutions, accounting firms, and law firms have an order-taking culture. Bankers are far more comfortable sitting behind a desk, waiting for the business to come to them.

They don't like to make sales calls. It's scary, and maybe they feel it's a little undignified. "People should know how good we are," they think to themselves. So they wait.

Your bankers will find every reason to do other "more important" things first.

2. You're not mining your existing customer base.

Calling on current customers is like picking low-hanging fruit.

Your bankers already know them. It's a lot easier to ask a current customer for a meeting. This must be a priority.

You should be scheduling yearly or twice-yearly consultations with business and high-value retail customers to find out how you can help them with new or future needs. (Please don't just drop in. That sends the message that you don't respect their time.)

3. You're not asking for referrals.

Satisfied customers will tell others about your bank. That's the kind of word of mouth that's nice, but passive. If you really want to cultivate new business leads, you must have an intentional effort at developing referrals.

Turn your failed officer-calling program into an A+, It's easy as 1-2-3:
1. Go to your customers' offices with coffee or treats in hand.
2. Ask them about how things are going—then listen.
3. Offer suggestions on bank products that will help them.
Bonus points if you can make suggestions that have nothing to do with your bank but that assist the customers in growing their businesses.

We recommend creating a well-branded, one-page marketing piece. It should explain what kinds of business you're looking for and how the referral source can help. It should be specific. Include details about the type of business, its attributes, its location, and so on.

You absolutely have to ask.

Then be sure to call the people recommended to you, follow up with the referral source, and report back. Thank everyone. Then thank them again.

As a leader, you know the passive approach is not enough to take your institution to the next level.

Some people will never overcome their trepidation over making sales calls. Especially cold ones. You may need to hire a hunter to make the cold calls and to do the work that brings in new business. But don't do it unless you've first implemented the steps above.

It's your job to lead. Your current staff can—and should—be able to grow more business through cultivating current customers. Help them move from an F to A++.

BIG, BAD WOLVES ARE NOT REAL—AND THERE ARE NO SILVER BULLETS

The monster lurking around the corner isn't the economy or absence of an advertising budget. It's a lack of strategy that keeps you from achieving your business-development goals.

While Jack had magic beans, you don't.

Branded swag, a fancy marquee, and forty locations do you no good whatsoever if you don't have a proactive, well-planned, business-development effort.

Here are five steps to get you on the right path:

1. **Stop talking about a CRM, and get one in place.** (We see this in both small and large institutions.) You can use a system with bells and whistles, like Salesforce, or you can create an in-house database that's sharable. *Don't you dare hand out another set of measuring cups with your logo until you have a database in place.*

2. **Set measurable goals.** Let all in your institution know what to shoot for and how they must help. Be the Pied Piper. Inspire and bring them all along with you, and you'll become an unstoppable force.

3. **Make sure you're not leaving money on the table.** Are renewals of lines of credit, overdraft protection, or safe deposit boxes languishing because of your inattention? Fee income is hard to come by. Make sure you're realizing the revenue from what you already have in place.

4. **Institute a service culture.** Do all your customers take advantage of products and services you offer—that they really need? If not, you should be having significant conversations with them. (In person.) Listen, then recommend.

5. **Get out of the bank.** Emailing prospects may make you feel like you're accomplishing something, but those emails are buried as easily as a pea under a mattress. Work your database. Pick up the phone. Call. Set appointments, then go listen. Bankers who make house calls are rare, so it's not that hard to set yourself apart.

Stop wasting time looking for the magic genie that makes business materialize. That's just for kids. Dig deep inside yourself and find the guts to meet giant goals head-on. Go slay them.

BREAK THE ICE: FOUR WAYS TO BETTER COLD CALLS

Whether you're growing customers, pitching a reporter, or recruiting board members, you have to make some asks. It can be uncomfortable.

But to advance your objectives, you've gotta brave the cold.

Here are four ways to make those efforts less frosty and more productive.

1. Make sure your database is in order, then use it.

Unfortunately, this bears repeating. Some organizations have excellent databases full of information about their prospects: likes and dislikes, last conversations, purchase history, past connection to the organization, and contacts received. Do not—I repeat—do not make a call without first reading what's in the database.

> Don't make people feel like last week's half-moldy leftovers by calling them without having a clue about them or their business.

If you don't have a database, implement one immediately. Employee turnover in many organizations is a constant. Merely keeping paper files or information committed only to memory means important institutional knowledge (and relationships) will be lost if an employee leaves.

2. Ask for an introduction, then call right away.

Who are the people on your "A list"? How do you gain or enhance connections with them? An easy start: see who you have in common on LinkedIn, then ask your connection to make an introduction. Be specific in your request. Tell why you want to meet the person your connection knows, and how the connection can help you. Once that introduction is made, follow up quickly before there's time for a chill to set in. Call your prospect (now you can name-drop) and ask for a meeting.

Afterward, be sure to close the loop with the person who helped you connect. Say thank you, and give a short report on how your conversation went.

Offer to return the favor.

Make it about them, not you.

Reporters

Frame your conversation about what's in his interest. Read his past stories. Know his angles. Why will his readers care about this? How will your pitch make his job easier?

Customers

What have they purchased from you in the past? Did you make a presentation, but not win their business? Why—and is it time to try again? Or if they did purchase, is it time for an upgrade or an add-on?

Call first thing in the morning or late in the day.

I've found that once the day gets rolling, it's harder to break through to people for anything, let alone an introductory call. They get into the swing of their hefty TO-DO list and are not open to unplanned interruptions.

But call them while they're still organizing their day—or winding down for tomorrow—and it may be the opportune time to talk. Plan for a short conversation... just enough

to establish a time to have a longer conversation by phone or over coffee. (Don't forget time zone differences and plan accordingly.)

Implement a better system to ask, and watch your organization's results catch fire!

BETTER BUSINESS DEVELOPMENT STARTS WITH HEARTBURN

When a business-development team gets charged up and ready to call on prospects, they're often so eager to talk that they forget to find out about what's keeping the prospects up at night.

Leading with what you have to offer is wasting that precious appointment you finally booked.

Start with your prospect's pain, and you'll have a much more productive conversation.

Why? Because the conversation is about them—and what you can actually do to help with their particular situation.

Here are four ways to research before you go in:

1. Gain knowledge from similar customers.

Of course you must be highly confidential about your other business relationships. But if you spend a little time mapping out the trends you see in particular groups of customers, you can spot some nuggets:

- Are others in the same industry struggling with financing equipment?
- Will the new tax laws affect their businesses—for better, or worse?
- Is foreign competition eroding their margins?
- You get the idea.

2. Get input from centers of influence.

Ask your advisory board members. What do your other referral sources say? Their knowledge of what's happening with their peers is likely deeper than yours. Ask them for help with background:

- What do they hear on the street?
- What's the discussion in their circles?

Listen for information and insights.

3. Get comfortable with social media.

A lot of bankers are reluctant to be active on social media. Get over it. You need to be on Facebook, LinkedIn, and any other places where your customers are active.

Watch the social media accounts for the business and its key people. These will give you more information on what they're pursuing, new

> Diagnose the prospect's problem before offering your remedy. That feels better already.

challenges, and opportunities.

- How are their customers interacting with them?
- Are there reviews?

There's a wealth of knowledge there. Use it.

4. Put the search engines to work.

Search the company and its competitors. Find out more about:

- Its key people
- Its trade associations
- Its reputation on employment websites

You can also access D&B and others, like LexisNexis. If your institution doesn't subscribe to these, your local business librarian does.

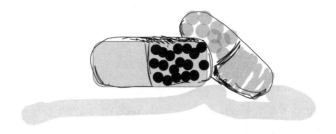

Does your customer need an antacid? Bring it!

Resist the temptation to go in with your Band-Aid. Bring solutions that address the source of the heartburn, and you'll develop a healthier and happier (and more profitable) relationship.

STOP TALKING ABOUT A SALES FUNNEL AND THINK OF IT AS A CHAIN

Old-school sales guys will tell you sales is just a numbers game.

Get enough prospects into the funnel, and they'll dump out X percent of customers at the bottom. Easy.

News flash, Herb Tarlek, your lack of a system is as outdated as your plaid polyester coat.

Here are three problems we see on a regular basis in attracting business accounts. Are you guilty?

You're OK with "spray and pray."

Not clearly defining the target audience, its demographics, wants, and needs—and how your product helps it—results in wasting a lot of time chasing people who don't care, can't afford your brand, or are simply not a good fit with your bank.

Think of your audience as an individual, rather than

a faceless group. What does she care about? Where is she? What's her daily life like? When you know those things, you have a better chance for a real conversation and a solution.

Your chain has broken links.

Everyone in your organization is part of the sales process, whether you realize it or not. If your business-development people are turning prospects over to treasury management, IT, loan officers, or another department without staying in the conversation, there's a potentially huge pitfall.

Do your support and CSR people know the correct answers to your prospect's concerns? Do they know how to position your bank against the competition? If you don't know what they're saying, stop right now and find out. They could be a weak or dangerously broken link.

You don't have a real system.

I got pulled through a really good sales system recently. It was impressive. I didn't feel as if I was being "sold"; rather, I felt as if they 1) respected my time, 2) cared about my needs, and 3) were speaking to me with a unified voice.

There was a one-two-three series of emails, an easy "click to schedule a phone call," and a fast response when I asked for references. My later conversation with someone in another department yielded consistent answers to my concerns.

And, there was good, friendly follow-up a week later, when I hadn't yet made a decision.

I'm going to assume that, by now, you have a CRM. If you don't, then get that on your list. First.

If you're not bringing in the new clients you'd hoped to bring in, it's time to reevaluate what you're doing.

Many institutions focus on their sales funnel and how much they can dump in at the top. But they fail to think about the entire process. Get a branded protocol in place, educate all your employees throughout the entire organization, and watch your sales results flourish.

WHY A SALES CONTEST CAN PUT YOUR BRAND ON DANGEROUSLY THIN ICE

Last week at a social event, I spoke with a man who works at a regional bank. I asked about his job, and he shocked me by saying, "I hate it!" Then he told me that he and his associates are pressured to sell additional products to customers and that he feels it's "immoral to try and sell them things they don't need." Yes, he said, "Immoral."

This is frighteningly thin ice—especially for a financial brand.

He doesn't know me that well, but he was very open in telling me how he felt about the job, the sales contests, and his employers' expectations.

This is a bright, friendly, and well-connected person. The kind of person many employers would love to have as a valued team member and an ambassador—not a detractor—of their brand.

This financial institution needs a program, not a sales contest. Here are four elements that make the difference between a high-performance program and a short-lived sales contest.

1. Everyone must be in on the business plan.

If all the people inside the institution understand the business goals—and their important individual roles in achieving those goals—they feel important and empowered. They will be ready and excited about rising to the challenge.

It's your job to make sure that they have goals and that they hear it from you. Keep the reinforcement going. Listen for feedback, then keep them in the loop. Leaving out this important element will have a chilling effect on all your efforts.

Ask

- Do my employees know the goals and specifically how each of them can help us get there?

- Do we have a rallying cry that includes and encourages everyone on our team?

- Are we keeping them in the loop on our efforts and our progress?

2. You inspire belief and love for your brand and purpose.

You need to inspire—because, let's face it, your institution offers most of the same things your competition does. What really sets you apart? Great service and a promise to remember customers' names aren't it.

Know your purpose, and have a mission and a vision that go beyond a forgettable plaque in the lobby.

Are you about small business? Or is your purpose Dave Ramsey-esque—helping people be more financially responsible? Are you young-family-focused or are you the go-to for agriculture?

Live it. Recruit for it, and don't settle. If your sales efforts are aligned with your brand and purpose, employees will understand the "why." They won't feel as if they're compromising their deeply held personal values. That puts you on solid ground.

Ask

- Does our brand live beyond the slogan on our mugs and the website?

- Can all our employees tell what's different about us, and do they help us communicate that through every touch point to each other and to everyone they meet?

3. You train on consultative selling.

Arm twisting and haranguing can create some short-term sales. But, in the end, employees and customers alike will be dissatisfied. It will be repeated throughout social media, at the PTO, and at local social events.

Employees need training on how to suggest products *only* after asking questions and listening intently. That gives them confidence to make recommendations that truly make a difference in the customer's life. That's the stuff of personal satisfaction in a job well done.

Ask

- Do we have an ongoing training program that helps everyone inside our institution confidently ask questions, listen, and recommend?

- Do we merely have an order-taking culture, where employees are afraid to ask?

- Or, worse yet, does our culture make employees feel like reluctant, used sweeper salespeople?

4. Employees have the technology tools to do their jobs.

Most institutions have CRM modules that let bankers see their customer relationships with the click of a mouse.

And many of those same institutions aren't fully using their technology.

Customer-service representatives should readily see important account profile information while conducting a transaction. That makes it much easier for them to start conversations that lead to better solutions for the customer and the bank.

> We've seen over and over again the negative impact of a culture that makes employees feel compelled to cheat. Don't let this happen to you.

But, really, it's not just up to CSRs. Anyone working with a customer can be using these tools more effectively.

Ask

- Are we invested in technology, and are we using it to its utmost?

- Do all the employees have the proper access to it so they can do what we have asked them to do?

Are you building sales or just selling?

Getting deeper, stickier relationships for your financial institution is the key to acquiring loyal, profitable customers. It all seems so simple: incentivize employees to cross-sell and let 'em go. But if you don't have a strong program—with effective training—you're veering into very dangerous territory.

SHHHH! STOP USING THE *S* WORD

Many bankers struggle with getting all of their staffers to feel confident with business development. That's because staffers are afraid of the *S* word.

Don't tell them to SELL; teach them to LISTEN.
Use our "Business-and-Baby" rule
as your internal rallying cry.

> Ask what's near and dear to their hearts.

The business-and-baby rule.
Nearly everyone has a business or
a baby. For some, the business is the
baby. For others, it's their pet. Or maybe the baby is her sports
car. The baby is simply what they love.

When you greet a customer, don't talk about the weather or
how busy you are. Instead, ask a question about the customer's
business or her baby. When you ask with interest, she'll light up.

Once she starts talking, listen for clues:

Is the business celebrating an anniversary?

Ask about future expansion or succession planning; then
think about financial products that can make those things
easier.

Is the child going to need college?

Ask about what he wants to be when he grows up; then think
about ways to help fund that future need with today's invest-
ments and offer that information.

**Is everyone at home missing work or school and using lots
of Nyquil?**

This is a prime time to talk about the benefits of an HSA.

Biz dev isn't just for loan officers—it's for everyone.
Selling is hard. Listening—then recommending something
that helps a customer—is really pretty easy.

Teach your staff that if they listen, customers will let them
know what they need. The rest is just about being helpful. That's
win-win, baby!

FOUR WAYS TO SELL WITHOUT SELLING OUT

All high-growth companies want to continue to grow sales and profits. And whether "sales" is in their title or not, you must get everyone throughout the organization to offer more to customers. Here are four examples from other industries that offer inspiration for win-win help—not just selling stuff people don't need.

1. Include them in an exclusive group.

Several high-performing credit unions I know offer seminars throughout the year to their members. Once they get to know these members, they offer small, exclusive group meetings, where members with complementary and noncompeting interests can come together to share ideas and support each other in their efforts. The group meetings are facilitated by a consultant or an expert. The institution offers it free to members and charges a small fee to prospects.

Win-win-win. The small-group setting is a special benefit to the members, while the consultant generates income and publicity. And the institution is viewed as a valuable connector.

2. Ask the right questions.

Some financial institutions routinely have a yearly "checkup" with their clients. Asking questions such as:

- When did you last update your will?

- Should we review your insurance coverage to be sure you have enough?

- Do key family members know where you keep your safe deposit box key?

When they have a genuine conversation—with lots of listening—good recommendations that benefit both parties will naturally follow.

Everybody wins. It's easy to sell if you think about what the client really needs.

3. Demonstrate with a little "show biz."

There's a local hair salon that also sells cosmetic products. After a haircut and a style, the stylist ushers the client over to the cosmetics area and refreshes her makeup at no charge... of course, with products the salon sells. It's oh-so-easy to add on a lipstick or other product to the ticket. And the client leaves the salon looking—and feeling—like a million dollars.

Extra credit: she's a radiant brand ambassador, as she puts her best face (and hair) forward.

How can you translate this concept to what you do in your institution?

4. Reach across departments.

One financial institution we know schedules a twice-yearly check-in with its business clients. The day-to-day account manager brings along someone from the C-suite, and, together, they talk about what the client needs now—and what pressures that client is feeling for the future. This deep conversation opens up dialogue that's often missed in the daily work.

The presence of the C-level person makes the client feel important, because he's getting extra attention from the top. And, finally, in that meeting, the client is asked who else at his organization should be approached. A recommendation from the "inside" to another department is often much better received than a cold call. It's a good way to make new business inroads within a large organization.

Make it part of your protocol.

These techniques fit institutions of all sizes. And they really work with daily focus and action. After all, whether you're focused on retail or business customers, great selling is personal.

- Brainstorm; then introduce additional product offerings (like the exclusive groups) that benefit customers.

- Train employees on how to ask questions, counsel, and help. Then reward them for doing it successfully.

- Be sure that whatever you're doing is honestly aligned with your brand essence and purpose.

Make smart cross-selling part of your everyday way of doing business, and it won't really feel like selling.

STRATEGIC ALLIANCES EXPAND YOUR REACH–AND YOUR VALUE–TO CUSTOMERS

When was the last time you thought about putting your well-known contacts and customers together to bring more value to everyone? As a banker, you know lots of people. Are you using that knowledge to expand your reach?

It's time to step back and think about how you can help others with more innovation and less "banking as usual."

Who are some people or organizations that are a natural match with each other? Here are a few to get you started.

1) Tax Professionals

Why?

Tax laws are often changing in significant ways. Just a few examples:

- Home equity loan interest: experts are still wrestling with what is or isn't tax deductible.
- Mortgage interest deductions are up and down.
- Medical expense deductions are changing.
- Leasing versus buying equipment has tax consequences.

What?

Could you partner with a tax professional now to offer some educational seminars or website articles to your customers and your bankers?

The Benefits

This is an opportunity to find better ways to serve your customers and to offer different deposit and loan products that help you both be more profitable. And the CPAs may gain some new clients, as well.

2) Marketing Professionals

Why?

Many small business owners struggle to keep on top of their marketing—especially when it comes to their social media. Many also have difficulty developing an integrated, budgeted marketing plan, so strategic planning falls by the wayside. They throw things at the wall to see what sticks. They're wasting money and slowing their growth.

What?

Invite a marketing firm (hopefully your customer) to give a "Low Cost Marketing" or a "Social Media 101" lunch-and-learn to your small business customers.

The Benefits

Small business customers who are spending more wisely and growing properly will grow with you. And while your small business customers may be too small to hire that marketing firm now, they may grow into a bigger, better business who can afford that firm later. They'll need more of your services, too. This is an effective way to build loyalty that lasts a long time.

Who else can be a smart referral connection?

Here are a few more ideas:

- Car dealers, farm-implement dealers, or fleet-leasing agents
- Architects and builders
- Specialty physician groups
- Fitness clubs, dance studios, and personal trainers

Take a little time to brainstorm with your team to see where other potential strategic alliances could be developed.

Make a list; then give your ideas the WHO/WHY/WHAT/ BENEFIT test.

One more benefit.

When your bankers have the benefit of these trainings, they're more knowledgeable. They'll be able to talk more confidently about the bank's products and do a credible job making recommendations to customers.

Dive in.

Once you have your list together, it's time for action creating your program.

- Set key dates.
- Determine who owns the responsibility.
- Know who will follow up.
- Decide how you'll measure.
- Do you need to test?
- Go!

There's no time like the present to build a pool of alliances and valuable resources for your institution and customers. Your better bottom line is waiting.

FOR THE WIN: MAKE YOUR CUSTOMERS LOOK GOOD TO THEIR CUSTOMERS

Many community financial institutions say they're customer-centric, yet they have a brand promise too focused on the bank. What if your brand difference is about helping your customers win with *their* customers?

That would merit some roaring fans. Here's how:

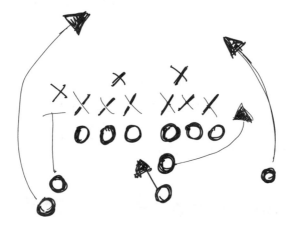

The finances are basic block and tackle.

We're going to assume that, by now, you already know how to listen, to diagnose, and to offer customers the best approach to achieving their growth.

To win, you need more. Help them do a better job serving their customers.

Presenting different models of how to structure the loan in the company's best interest is good service and important. *Yet any of your worthy competitors can do that, too.*

It's not enough to say you'll help them with financing or ways to be more profitable. That's basic block and tackle.

Find out what their customers need.

As a financial institution, you can't address everything your customers need. But it's fair to say that if you listen and do a little research, you can come up with some solid products that benefit everyone.

Here are some examples to get you started:

Is your customer a retailer gearing up for a key sales season?

You could help develop a layaway program that lets shoppers choose their purchases up front, then pay in installments until the appointed time. The layaway model of years ago is enjoying a resurgence among budget-conscious families. Help your customer benefit from this trend.

Does your customer employ a lot of entry-level staffers at a lower pay scale—or even employees who are unbanked?

You could help with:

- A pay-card solution
- Financial literacy lunch-and-learns
- Easy-to-open basic accounts at their place of business (employees can sign up on break)

A less-stressed, more financially confident employee benefits your customer tremendously.

Does your customer serve young families?

Offer this customer a way to create a copromotion that gives a US Savings Bond or starter savings account for her children. This could be tied to a promotion or as a benefit to VIPs. That's an up-sell opportunity that can help your customer grow.

Get creative and be a problem solver for your customers.

Go for the win-win-win. Help your customers win with their customers, and everyone cheers!

THREE SIDES OF A COIN: HACKING BUSINESS DEVELOPMENT

Think about the problem you're working on. State it here. (Example: I want to sell more safe deposit boxes, or I want to open more new SBA loans.)

Let's turn it over and over.

Think of a solution previously suggested (by yourself or another) to which you said, *"Nope, it won't work."*

1) Make a case that supports the solution that you just said won't work.

_____

_____

_____

_____

_____

_____

_____

2) What is the flip side of the solution you just supported? Make a case for that approach.

_____

_____

_____

_____

_____

_____

3) Hack the problem. (For example, I can't sell more services, but I could *rent* them, sell *subscriptions* to them, *bundle* them with someone else's product, and so forth.)

_____

_____

_____

_____

_____

_____

What did you discover? Were there some answers you didn't expect? Do some merit further exploration? What's next?

_____

_____

_____

_____

_____

_____

_____

INNOVATE OR DIE

"*Without tradition, art is a flock of sheep without a shepherd.
Without innovation, it is a corpse.*"
—WINSTON CHURCHILL

"*The heart and soul of the company is creativity and innovation.*"
—BOB IGER, CHAIRMAN & CEO OF WALT DISNEY

"*Trust the young people; trust this generation's innovation.
They're making things, changing innovation every day. And all
the consumers are the same: they want new things, they want
cheap things, they want good things, they want unique things. If
we can create these kind of things for consumers, they will come.*"
—JACK MA, COFOUNDER AND CEO OF THE ALIBABA GROUP

"*New products, new markets, new investors,
and new ways of doing things are the lifeblood of growth.
And while each innovation carries potential risk, businesses
that don't innovate will eventually diminish.*"
—ADENA FRIEDMAN, PRESIDENT & CEO OF NASDAQ

INNOVATION OPERATION

While many think creativity has to do only with being able to draw a stick figure, I'm a firm believer that it's really about solving a problem in a new way.

Creativity takes mental muscle, and it requires discipline, training, and practice. It means saying no to multitasking and breaking up with some bad habits.

So, to set the tone for this chapter, build some habit-breaking exercises into your coming week. These will help you be more mindful of the present and make some new observations.

First order of business: break up with multitasking.

Multitasking is sometimes a necessary evil. There are many things competing for our attention. Most seem urgent. But what's really an emergency, and what is actually just noise?

Schedule some time today—and in the coming week—to take an intentional break from multitasking. Check a box each time you do it. See what new (better) habits you can develop.

Create some quiet.

Don't be like Pavlov's dog. If you automatically check email and social media as soon as you hear the notification, you're hooked. Mute those notifications, and check them only once an hour. In all but the rarest cases, it's all that's necessary.

Listen between the lines.

When you're on a phone call: don't sneakily check email or surf the web while you listen. Give your undivided attention to the person talking with you and learn more. (If you're tempted, talk via Facetime or Skype so the other person can see you.) When you're fully mindful of the other person, it's surprising what you will discover.

Don't eat at your desk.

Snarfing down lunch while reading the news or checking email is a disservice to your brain. Get up and go! Hit the library, a park, or a museum. Notice the food and your surroundings. Even if you take only twenty minutes, you'll return to your office refreshed.

Feel free to doodle.

Perhaps counterintuitively, doodling while listening in a meeting has been proven to help people focus and retain more. Take a packet of colored pencils or Sharpies to the next meeting and find out.

Watch for more as you read on. Be ready to try some new things on for size.

PUT DOWN THE APPLE: A STICKY DILEMMA

One sunny fall afternoon, I cut a bright green apple into six slices and placed them on the deck railing outside my office for the local squirrels to enjoy. Almost immediately, a hungry, little squirrel appeared, obviously delighted with his find.

He was so delighted, in fact, that he picked up as many pieces as his greedy little arms could hold. The problem: there were still two pieces of apple remaining on the railing.

His little brain spun. What to do? He couldn't pick up the other pieces that he wanted so badly. He couldn't run off to his nest, because he was overloaded with what he already had.

It was a sticky problem, and he was paralyzed with indecision. Would he forego opportunity for security? Would he starve while trying to make a decision?

We'll never know. I had to get back to work.

But this image has never left me. It's a reminder to us humans to ask ourselves: what's paralyzing us because we're afraid to put something down? And is this hoarding keeping us from making progress on important issues? Will we "starve"?

Write down three things that might be paralyzing you. Give them ten minutes of attention each day for the next week.

What do you need to put down so you can pick up something that will feed you far into the future?

1) _____

2) _____

3) _____

Indecision not only hampers productivity; it can cost you great opportunities.

As industrious as squirrels are, I'm guessing he figured that out. You can, too.

BUSINESS SPAGHETTI: STOP WAITING TO SEE WHAT STICKS

"Things change so fast, there's no room for a plan," we've heard more than once—from more than one CEO. They don't want to be tied down, so they throw out random tactics and wait to see what sticks. Here are three ways to be ready for change, while you're still working on a smart plan for your institution's future.

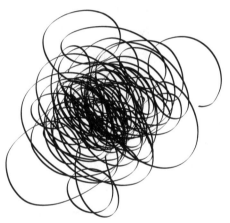

1. Allocate budget for experimentation.

Set aside some budget for trying out new tactics. If they're grounded in good research and strategy, you can be smart and find satisfaction in the shininess of it all.

Measure. If the experiment turns out to be a flop, you haven't sacrificed much money or your market share. If it's successful, then you have a well-founded reason to alter your course.

2. Allow for brand extensions or product enhancements.

Having a plan and sticking to it doesn't mean that you can't add features and benefits that customers want. In fact, every good strategic plan has room for the improved—and maybe even the "brand-new."

Devote quality time listening to employees, customers, and suppliers about what's missing. What will make their lives better, easier, or more fulfilling? Find out; then feed your need for some razzle-dazzle by making your offerings even more enticing.

3. Don't be the bad example.

Be disciplined with yourself. If you're modeling different behavior than you say you want, people will emulate what they see. If you're guilty of not living up to the company vision, expect others to be guilty, too.

As the leader, it's up to you to create a vision and a purpose, then to build a culture of employees who are eager to help you get there. Share your ideas, and be open to your team's thoughts on how to make those ideas even better than what you came up with on your own. (And be generous in giving credit to others, when those ideas blossom.)

Be proactive instead of reactive.

Experimentation in the right circumstances brings innovation. In the wrong circumstances, it makes a mess.

Throwing something against the wall to see what sticks may be fun, but it's no way to run a high-performance business. Be proactive instead of reactive, and watch the profits grow.

DON'T "NICE" YOURSELF OUT OF PROFITABILITY

A bank president recently told me he lets safe deposit box

rent-renewal notices slide, because he hates to bug people over something so small and he wants to be nice.

It made me wonder whether he's really nice or just afraid to risk irritating a customer over a relatively small fee.

Either way, there are three important questions to ask:

1. What message does this send to employees—and does this make it OK for them to avoid the sometimes uncomfortable task of speaking to someone about a fee?

2. Do customers even know they're receiving this "favor," and do they value it?

3. How much income is diverted from the bottom line because of these actions (or lack thereof) and the repercussions?

We all know that financial institutions need fee income—and they need customer loyalty. So it's important to balance great customer service with charging appropriate fees.

Help good customers.

Some institutions waive the occasional overdraft fee for a good customer. After the initial embarrassment, the customer gratefully accepts—and appreciates—the bank's generosity. That can help solidify the relationship. But you don't do it for anyone and everyone.

Model good behavior to employees.

The bigger issue is what this president is modeling for his staff. If they're uncomfortable with fees and they see the leadership act as if fee income isn't important, that's what they'll believe.

Show them the right way to do things.

Evaluate your procedures.

While safe deposit box rentals won't make or break you, they do represent recurring revenue that's not always easy to generate. Take a look at your operations and your procedures: where are other areas you may be letting potential revenue evaporate? Find those holes and fill them appropriately.

> Being nice is only an added value if people want it and are aware you gave it to them.

Take action.

Once you have an accurate picture of the leakage, implement the action needed to stop it. Set deadlines, assign roles, then see how easily you've developed more revenue. Nice!

GET OUT OF YOUR OWN WAY: THREE OBSTACLES TO INNOVATION THAT START WITH YOU

Too many CEOs are looking for growth but can't seem to get out of their current rut. Their greatest obstacle? Themselves.

Here are three common examples and how to obliterate them.

1. Living in the trenches.

As the leader, it's up to you to establish a vision and clear goals, then to trust your employees to carry the business forward. It's fun to roll up your sleeves and share camaraderie with the troops. But that hands-on work can easily become a distraction that takes your focus away from the big picture of casting vision and leading your bank.

You need to be above the fray to see what's really happening. That's what allows you to forecast, to evolve, and to keep your brand relevant in a tumultuous marketplace.

2. Failing to listen.

Decisions made based on gut instinct alone—or worse, the shiny *objet du jour*—are likely to fail. Listen to your employees, your customers, and your trusted advisors; then make a decision that's well-grounded in facts.

Don't let your gut dictate how you make important decisions. Sure, give a little credence to those gut feelings. But if you allow them free rein, you'll just end up with painful ulcers and falling profits.

3. Analysis paralysis.

It's smart to analyze before making big decisions. But, at some point, you need to take a leap of faith. Know the facts, make a decision, and move ahead. Spending a lot of time examining minutia may start to feel like important work. But be wary: if it's really an excuse to delay a decision, you are in trouble.

You will always deal with some amount of risk. It's your job to manage and to mitigate. The longer you wait, the more momentum you lose—and the further ahead your competitors will be.

Are you holding yourself back?

Take some time to examine how well you're performing

against your plan. If you're missing goals, you may need help getting out of your own way.

HOW A RIDE-ALONG INSPIRES INNOVATION AND SALES

What could you learn if you and your employees really rode along on your customer's journey?

It can definitely build your brand.

Here's how to learn more and to get profits speeding ahead.

How do others really experience your brand?

After a recent hectic day of shopping, I stopped at a famous coffee shop for a pick-me-up. I wanted to make a stop in the ladies room, and since I was alone, I had to take my coat, handbag, and packages with me. As I entered the tiny, dimly lit space, I searched in vain for a place to hang my coat. I wished for a countertop to park my parcels on, and I grumbled to myself: "I wish the architect of this establishment would have to try out this restroom like I am right now." (Yes, it was a curse.)

It got me thinking about how customer experiences everywhere are often goldmines waiting to be discovered, if only someone digs. Brands can be tremendously improved by your simply creating a route to help them journey into the unknown.

Don't merely survey your customers, because they don't always remember if it's not fresh in their minds. Observe them in action.

Hit the pavement!

Business Customers

- Go visit your customer in his factory to see how his product is made.

- Attend a trade show and observe how he responds to his competition.
- Shadow along on some sales calls.

Find out his challenges, his wins and losses, and what happens in his business on a daily basis.

Walk in his shoes, and I guarantee you'll be better positioned to offer him services he really needs—not just what you think he needs. And, yes, you will both increase sales and profits.

Retail Customers

- Actually go through the steps of opening an account online or on paper at one of your branches.
- Open up a statement and read how much insider language is noted there.
- Go outside and watch what happens at the drive-up window.
- Try to set up your online banking app from scratch or to assist someone who hasn't done it yet.
- Go into one of your branches and use the restroom that's reserved for your customers.

Observe what the experience feels like, how long it takes, and whether it's pleasant, fun, or ridiculously frustrating.

Include employees on these trips.

This exercise isn't just for you. Now that you've seen the potential ROI, get your employees involved, too. Send them on ride-alongs with:

- Customers
- Employees in other departments
- Suppliers

Create a forum for employees to share what they've learned through your intranet, staff meetings, and other gatherings.

What have you learned?

1. You'd observe some opportunities for product improvements that help customers in new ways and that distance your brand from the competition.
2. You'd (hopefully) have even greater pride in the work your institution does, as you see how it changes another person's life.
3. You'd have empathy and a stronger sales presentation, smarter marketing materials, and better-trained employees.
4. You'll increase sales and profits.

Soon, a new perspective can spread throughout your entire organization. A culture of innovation and action will prevail. Profits will naturally race ahead.

HOW HONEYBEES AND JACKALOPES CAN SPUR INNOVATION

While the word "innovation" is almost ubiquitous, the ability to come up with new ideas that are truly groundbreaking seems to be anything but. Enter honeybees and jackalopes—and how they can lend a hand.

Accidental Cross-Pollination

Bees typically gather nectar and pick up pollen all from the same apple tree. But apple trees need cross-pollination: pollen from one tree must fertilize a different tree. We can't wait around and hope for a bee to accidentally end up on a different

tree. What we can count on is that bees will later mix with each other and inadvertently transfer the pollen they've picked up to other bees. Those bees are the important link in growing new apples.

The lesson for hopeful innovators

Cross-pollinate. Don't hang out with the same people all the time. Get outside your office. Invite people from different departments and different companies to help. Be sure to include frontline employees who probably have excellent perspective on needs that aren't being met.

If you make new friends and create new alliances, you'll get the chance to brush up against some other ideas that would work really well when they transfer to what you're working on.

Intentional Cross-Pollination

A jackalope isn't a real creature, but some people will swear it exists. It's said to be a hybrid of the pygmy deer and a species of killer rabbit.

The New York Times attributes the mythical creature's origin to a 1932 hunting-outing involving taxidermist Douglas Herrick. When he and his brother returned from a hunting trip for jackrabbits, Herrick tossed a carcass into the taxidermy store, where it came to rest beside a pair of deer antlers. The accidental combination of animal forms sparked the idea for a jackalope. The rest, as they say, is history.

The lesson for hopeful innovators

Mix it up. The Herricks' idea was sparked from an accidental pile of objects. You can purposely mix up some unlikely objects as an idea starter and see where it leads.

Expose yourself to different magazines, books, TV shows,

and movie genres than the ones you usually choose for yourself. If you normally participate in sports, try learning to draw or dance. Pretty soon, your brain will be connecting dots you haven't even seen before.

Some Cross-Pollination "WHAT IFs?"

• Product displays in a bank lobby (think boats or brides): bring to life what a loan can really do.

• Cheerleaders in a retirement home: create a festive, team-like atmosphere for residents, their families, and employees.

• Hostesses in a tech store: make stressed, bewildered customers feel relaxed and welcome.

• A "cap-and-trade" program in a club with attendance requirements: increases membership engagement and reduces turnover.

• Entertainment at a food-manufacturing facility: is actually training in disguise.

Two Rules of Thumb

1) Don't kill ideas before they get a chance to fly. Doug Hall of Eureka! Ranch says that the "virtual no" kills more ideas than anything else. Instead of no, say "what if?"

2) Keep an idea file. Get a sketchbook (either old-school or virtual) and save clippings, ideas, and photos that catch your attention. Scribble and make notes. Don't worry about categorizing or organizing. Just getting these interesting tidbits together in one place creates a deep well of inspiration when you need to work on something new.

Start now.

WAKE UP YOUR BRAIN: EXERCISE

In the week ahead, take the time to do some brain-awakening exercises on your own. Make them habits that help you see, hear, and experience things in new ways. Below are seven so that you can do one each day of the week. Repeat. Build some newfound brain habits.

1. Commute to work by a different route than usual: notice sights, sounds, smells, colors, textures, and faces. Mindfully say aloud what you notice.

2. Spend one hour doing things with your nondominant hand. Notice what's awkward and what's easy. If you're ambidextrous, do it blindfolded.

3. Eat dessert first.

4. Unplug and sit. Find a park bench and some quiet for ten minutes. Notice the clouds and amuse yourself by thinking of at least ten things their shapes resemble. No judging.

5. Reflect on your favorite childhood food. In your mind, enjoy its fragrance, texture, taste, and smell. Go get the real thing within the next twenty-four hours.

6. Listen to a TED talk selected at random: ted.com/talks

7. Peruse a magazine that's new to you (print or issuu.com). Let your mind wander. Notice the different photography and writing styles, designs, and ads. Consider how the ideas you see can inject new life into your:
   • Social media
   • Culture
   • Business plan

- Employee appreciation
- Customer development
- Board communications
- Public relations
- Promotional activities
- More

MORE GOLD, LESS GRAVEL: INTERNAL CROWDSOURCING

Wikipedia calls crowdsourcing "distributed problem solving: assigning a problem to a large group of people to mine collective intelligence." Many companies use crowdsourcing for product development. Doritos and numerous other advertisers have famously used it for commercials in the highest profile TV commercials in the country.

Is it for you?

Prospecting on the Down Low

Are you stuck somewhere? You may not be ready to let the masses work on an assignment for your institution—especially if you're in a rapid-growth environment, where you can't tip your hand to competitors or other outsiders. But a modified approach to crowdsourcing is right under your nose. Try it with internal audiences—employees, boards of directors, or suppliers—instead.

24K ideas

With traditional crowdsourcing, many participants are only partially familiar with your business or your challenge. So there's a lot of sifting to be done, because the crowd can deliver volumes of dirt and gravel that must be thrown out before the nuggets are discovered.

But if you start with internal audiences, you may come to some brilliant EUREKA! moments sooner. Internal audiences are working from a rock-solid foundation of product knowledge.

You could be stuck because you're asking the wrong questions. Internal audiences may change the questions. They'll have a different perspective and can help reframe or refocus to get at the heart of the matter.

Other advantages of asking internal customers:

Employees are in closer contact with customers.

They can be your eyes and ears. They hear about needs; they understand frustrations; and they probably already have ideas. They want to help move your institution forward. This can be substantive, rewarding work.

Suppliers are in contact with others in your industry.
They know about trends from a different perspective. They know where the bodies are buried. They will be a vital resource if you ask and listen.

Directors have a valued network and other business experiences to bring to the table.
They can help cross-pollinate by bringing outside ideas and helping reshape them into something relevant to your business.

Start Panning

Always state the desired objective. Provide a time frame and a budget. Share the vision; then get out of the way. Resist the urge to micromanage or to impose too many rules. Encourage and reward upside-down, inside-out thinking.

Here are some ideas to get started:

1. Create a cross-department innovation team for ongoing work. Include people from all levels and departments. Assign them one "big idea" per month supporting the objectives. Have a kick-off meeting; then let them go to work.

2. Build in some competition. Ask for multiple teams to work on the assignment. Cultivate friendly rivalry and team spirit—then idea-swap and have each team take the other's ideas to a new level.

3. Design a contest for a specific assignment: use your intranet and other internal communications tools to announce and promote the contest. Be clear that everyone is encouraged to participate. Set the ground rules and offer a glitzy prize.

4. Create virtual work groups on specific challenges, using an online collaboration tool like Basecamp. This works especially well for suppliers or directors who don't have a daily presence in your office, or for employees working in different locations.

Bold Rush

High-growth companies know fortune favors the bold. You've got a depth of talent and brains inside your bank. Rush forth to harness that power. You'll see increased internal engagement and love for your brand—and stronger performance at the bottom line.

OPEN-DOOR POLICY

If you keep the door closed, pretty soon the room gets stuffy.
Really stuffy.

When you open the door for others, you let in some fresh air and new ways to approach your solutions. You know this. But are you doing it?

Think about whom you need to invite in.

What types of people should you welcome?

- (Think age, culture, gender, part of town, industry, and so on.)

What roles can they play?

- (Think employee, mentor, assistant, advisory board member, coach, supplier.)

Are there some things you need to put behind you? What door or doors should you be closing?

_____

_____

_____

_____

_____

_____

_____

DON'T LEAVE EMPLOYEES (AND CUSTOMERS) IN THE DARK

Everyone is busy. Just ask someone at a cocktail party how things are going. Invariably, they say they're busy.

Like many high performers, your people may be running as fast as they can. The problem: somewhere along the line, they've been taught to mind their own book of business, not the business of the entire bank. When it comes to what's happening one floor above, they're in the dark.

We've seen multiple community banks that offer mortgages,

insurance, trust management, and other services that they rarely cross-sell.

You've become blind to the fact that you're leaving money on the table.

There could be several reasons.

- Those other departments are in different locations: out of sight, out of mind.

- Employees don't understand the other products well enough to confidently suggest them.

- You have incentivized employees on the basis of individual goals, not team or bank goals.

Open new doors with an in-house training series.

- Set a regular monthly time at lunch or early morning.
- Provide good food.
- Assign each product/department head a program date so they can prepare and conduct training sessions for their colleagues. (If you're bound by geography, do these by Skype or other tech so everyone can participate live.)
- Provide a "cheat sheet" for easy reference after the meeting.
- Share financial goals and some incentives: help employees see the difference they can make by helping educate customers about ALL your product offerings.

Set the tone.

This isn't about selling. It is about helping customers who already trust and love you learn more about services that can improve their lives or their businesses.

Business goals are everyone's goals.
Keep your customers front and center in break rooms, your intranet, and during regular staff meetings. Keep all employees apprised of progress, celebrate the wins, and watch greater revenue and profits flow to your bottom line.

LET'S GO

NOTES

NOTES